Study Guide to
Death of a Salesman
by Arthur Miller

by Ray Moore

Picture attribution

Arthur Miller (date unknown). This image is in the public domain being the work of a United States Department of State employee, taken or made as part of that person's official duties. (Source Wikimedia Commons)

Contents

Preface 1
Introduction 3
Guiding Questions 5
    Notes and Commentaries 5
    ACT ONE 5
    ACT TWO 30
    REQUIEM 54
Perspectives 58
Critical Analysis 59
    Dramatis Personae: Introduction to the Significant Characters 59
    Settings 65
    Genre 66
    Characterization 71
    Structure 88
    Themes 89
    Symbols 93
Literary Terms 97
    Literary Terms Activity 100
Graphic Organizers 102
    Plot 102
    Different perspectives 103
Reading Group Use of the Study Guide Questions 104
Bibliography 106
To the Reader 107

Preface

A study guide is an *aid* to the close reading of a text; it should never be a substitute for reading that text. This play deserves to be read reflectively, and the aim of this guide is to facilitate such a reading primarily through the Guiding Questions, which have no answers provided. This is a deliberate choice. The questions are for readers who want to come to their own conclusions about the text and not simply to be told what to think about it by someone else. Even 'suggested' answers would limit the exploration of the text by readers themselves which is my primary aim. In the classroom, I found that students frequently came up with answers that I had not even considered, and, not infrequently, that they expressed their ideas better than I could have done. The point of this guide is to *open up* the text, not to close it down by providing 'ready-made answers.' Teachers do not need their own set of predetermined answers in order effectively to evaluate the responses of their students.

In the Notes and Commentaries section, the notes briefly explain the most important of the historical and geographical references in the play, and the commentaries analyze the most significant points of each scene. They do not set out to answer the questions, but often they do cover some of the same ground. Each commentary represents my best understanding of a chapter at this point in time. The commentaries make no claim to be complete and certainly not to be definitive. Readers should take from them the interpretations with which they agree; refine the interpretations with which they do not fully agree; and replace with their own ideas the interpretations with which they disagree.

The Critical Analysis section is based upon wide reading of literary criticism on this play. My aim is to reflect the wide range of views among critics while offering a clear and consistent reading of the text. Again, feel free to disagree.

Acknowledgements

As always, I am indebted to the work of numerous reviewers and critics. Where I am conscious of having taken an idea or a quotation from a particular author, I have cited the source in the text and the bibliography. Any failure to do so is an omission which I will immediately correct if it is drawn to my attention.

I believe that all quotations used fall under the definition of 'fair use.' If I am in error on any quotation, I will immediately correct my text.

Thanks are due to my wife, Barbara, for reading the manuscript, for offering valuable suggestions, and for putting the text into the correct formats for publication. Any errors which remain are my own

Introduction

Plot Summary

The date is c.1949. Willy Loman is a sixty-three-year-old traveling salesman for the Wagner Company based in New York. He has worked for the company for thirty-four years, selling its products (we never learn what these are) to retailers throughout New England. For almost twenty-five years, Willy has lived with his wife Linda in Brooklyn where they have raised two sons: Biff (now thirty-four) and Happy (now thirty-two). Both sons have lived away from home for several years. Biff left home about fifteen years before after a long and bitter argument with Willy and has been drifting from job to job in the West for some years; Happy, who works in a junior position in selling, lives in his own apartment. Both sons have temporarily returned to the Brooklyn home for the first time in many years.

As the play opens, it is late Monday evening. Willy returns unexpectedly, having left that morning on a sales trip to Portland. It soon becomes clear that he is in the final stages of a mental breakdown. For some time, Willy's sales (which were never exceptional in the first place) have been in decline, and five weeks previously his boss, Howard Wagner, took him off salary, and he has been earning only commission, which does not bring in enough for him to meet his bills. Both of Willy's sons seem to be failures: Biff has been trying to 'find himself' ever since he left home, and Happy is stuck in a low-ranking and low-paying assistant position. All of Willy's hopes and dreams of being able to achieve success and make enough money to pass something tangible on to his sons seem to be crumbling. It is a far cry from fifteen years before when Biff was a star high school quarterback with scholarship offers from three universities and seemed to have a bright future in business ahead of him. The play, which covers the last twenty-four hours of Willy Loman's life (not including the Requiem), explores the reasons why Willy's dreams of making his fortune as a salesman and of teaching his sons (particularly Biff, who is his favorite) to achieve outstanding success in the business world are crumbling before his eyes.

Why Read this Book?

Although from the start there were a few dissenting voices, *Death of a Salesman* was well received by both reviewers and audiences when it premiered, in February 1949, on Broadway, where it ran for 742 performances. The play won the 1949 Pulitzer Prize for Drama, the New York Drama Critics Circle Award, and the Tony Award for Best Play. Since 1949, *Salesman* has been revived many times on television and film as well as on the stage, and there has scarcely be a time when it has not been performed somewhere in the world. Critics can (and do) disagree on the greatness of the play, on whether it is really a tragedy, on how convincing its characterization is, or on how coherently its themes are developed, but there can be no doubt that *Salesman* is amongst the most important and enduringly popular plays of the twentieth century.

Issues with this Text

There is some mild cursing and profanity in the dialogue.

Hostile critics often accuse Miller of being a Communist and the play of being a political attack on American capitalism. Leonard Moss writes that "[Miller] appeared in June 1956 before the House Committee on Un-American Activities [chaired by Senator Joseph McCarthy]. He testified that, although, he "had signed many appeals and protests issued by Red front groups in the last decade," he had never been "under Communist discipline" (8). Before the Committee, Miller stated that, while he "would not support now a cause dominated by Communists," he adamantly refused to name others who has similarly supported Liberal, Left Wing or Communist cases and groups. There is no doubt that Miller, like many artists of his generation, flirted with the ideology to which we give the names Communism, Socialism or Marxism. It is also evident that some of Karl Marx's criticisms of capitalism *are* present in the play. That said, *Salesman* is *not* political propaganda; it is a moving depiction of the disintegration of a man's dreams in a capitalist world, which is something very different.

[To be 'fair and balanced,' I recommend the following article: Kengor, Paul. "Arthur Miller – Communist." *The American Spectator*. 16 Oct. 2015. 25 Jul. 2018. Web.]

Guiding Questions

Miller divides the play into two acts within which the action is fluid and continuous. One scene flows seamlessly into the next so that it is occasionally difficult to specify exactly where one ends and the next begins. As a result, there is no general agreement on scene division. The divisions used below are my own. A short scene, called "Requiem," concludes the play.

The questions aim to focus your reading of the play, in order to help you to develop your understanding the text. They do not normally have simple answers, nor is there always one answer. Consider a range of possible interpretations – preferably by discussing the questions with others. Disagreement is encouraged!

Notes and Commentaries

The Notes aim to explain points in the text – particularly things that have become unclear over time. The Commentaries represent my best understanding of what is important in the text. Do not accept anything I write in them uncritically. Their aim is to stimulate your own ideas.

ACT ONE

Stage Directions ("A melody ..." to "... follow to their end.")

1. You will find it very helpful to sketch the stage set from the author's initial description. Be prepared to make additions and adjustments as the play progresses.
2. Explain the contrast between what the audience *hears* as the lights go up and what is *seen*.
3. How can Willy Loman *hear* the flute but not be *aware* of it? What do you think the author is getting at here?
4. Comment on the metaphor, "[Willy] thankfully lets his burden down."
5. Explain the basis of Linda's admiration for her husband.

Commentary

The audience hears a flute "*small and fine, telling of grass and trees and the horizon,*" but sees a crowded urban landscape: the "*small, fragile-seeming*" Loman house (note the similarity in the description of the house and the flute) is surrounded on all sides by the "*towering angular shapes*" of apartment houses. Thus, the basic opposition between the natural world of the great outdoors and the urban world of commerce and development is explicit from the start.

The Lomans belong to the lower-middle class. Home ownership is an essential aspect of the American Dream, and the Lomans have a two-bedroom home which has all of the usual appliances. When Willy bought the house it was in semi-rural Brooklyn, but in the twenty-five years since then, the city has encroached upon the green spaces so that now the "*small fragile-seeming home*" is oppressed by that "*solid vault of apartment houses.*" The word "vault" is carefully chosen for it has two relevant connotations: it suggests both a bank vault and a tomb. The former links the apartments with the world of business, investments and finance which has gradually entrapped the house and the people in it, and the latter suggests that something in the house has died.

We are told, "*An air of the dream clings to the place, a dream arising out of reality.*" What this means is unclear on first reading. In fact, the place is the locale of two incompatible dreams, both of which may be said to be based on different realities – the great outdoors which it once embodied and the sprawling city which is its present reality. This will become clearer as the play progresses.

We experience this conflict as Willy enters, "*The flute plays on. He hears but is not aware of it.*" Willy seems deaf to the flute and to all that it represents; it exists only in his subconscious having been repressed from his consciousness. We watch as Willy, "*thankfully lets his burden down.*" This refers to the two large suitcases of samples that he carries. (We never do learn what Willy sells, but some form of clothing and hosiery would be a reasonable guess.) The words "*thankfully*" and "*burden*" suggest that it is not the weight of the actual cases that exhausts Willy but the role of salesman that they symbolize and the weight of the many failures he has suffered in that role. For a few moments, when alone, he can be himself; the mask of salesman can be discarded.

Linda, we are told, "*more than loves [Willy] ... she admires him.*" In her husband, Linda sees a man who has "*massive dreams ... [and] turbulent longings*" of which she knows herself to be incapable. Unfortunately, her admiration for her husband (which amounts at times to awe) means that she is insufficiently critical of him. Again and again, she instinctively supports his distorted view of reality when she ought to confront him with the harsh truths.

Real Time Dialogue between Willy and Linda ("Linda: Willy!" to "Willy: I'll be right up.")

6. What do you find significant about Linda's reaction to her husband's unexpected return?
7. Willy is remarkably honest about the problems that he had driving, but Linda makes a series of excuses for him. List them.
8. How does Willy react to the fact that, as he was driving north, he found himself "observing the scenery"?
9. What is strange about Willy's statement that he "opened the windscreen and just let the warm air bathe over [him]"? [Clue: The play is set in the late 1940s. Look at some pictures of American cars from that decade.]
10. What reasons does Willy give to Linda for initially rejecting her suggestion

that he should talk again to his boss about a job in New York? Can you suggest (by close reference to the text) the real reasons why he does not want to do this? Why do you think he changes his mind?

11. Biff and Happy are obviously only visiting. Contrast the different reactions of Willy and Linda to the fact that their boys have grown up and left home.

12. There is evidently tension between Willy and Biff, his oldest son. Willy's attitude to Biff is full of contradictions. In two columns, make lists of his contradictory statements.

13. Why do you think that Willy gets so angry about the fact that Linda has bought a new kind of cheese?

14. In what ways has the neighborhood in Brooklyn changed since the Lomans first moved there? Who/what does Willy blame for these changes?

15. What is illogical about a salesman like Willy complaining that "There's more people!"? What can you infer from his cry, "Competition is maddening!"?

16. There is plenty of evidence in this dialogue that Willy is increasingly living in the past. Why do you think that he is doing this?

Notes

"Portland": The most populous city in the state of Maine and the biggest port in New England. The drive from Brooklyn to Maine is about 320 miles.

"Brown and Morrison": Appears to be a fictional retail store.

"Thomas Edison": Thomas Alva Edison (1847-1931) was a phenomenally successful American inventor and businessman. Edison described himself as being deaf, once claiming, "I have not heard a bird sing since I was twelve years old." This was something of an exaggeration.

"B. F. Goodrich": Benjamin Franklin Goodrich (1841-1888) was an American industrialist in the rubber industry. He founded the B. F. Goodrich Company in 1880, though it did not become successful until after his death.

Commentary

The real-time action of the play opens in 1949. Willy returns unexpectedly from a sales trip, evidently exhausted. Linda is immediately on edge. She asks if something happened and if he wrecked the car. These questions, and Willy's irritable response to them, suggest that this has happened before. Willy is totally honest and open about the reason for his return: he says he feels "tired to the death," an expression which foreshadows his thoughts of suicide (about which we only learn later); that he "suddenly couldn't drive anymore" (pretty much fatal to the career of a traveling salesman); that he could not keep his mind on driving and kept drifting onto the shoulder of the road; and that he "absolutely forget I was driving." Willy will never be so honest again in the entire play: he realizes that something is seriously wrong with him. Symbolically, Willy's inability to steer the car (that quintessential symbol of American success and of the modern world) represents the fact that he is no longer in control of his life.

Strangely Linda (who we later discover already knows that her husband has attempted several times to kill himself and fears that he will do so again) provides him with excuses: maybe the steering on the car is off again because the mechanic is unfamiliar with the Studebaker; maybe Willy needs new glasses; perhaps Willy just needs to "rest" his mind because it is "overactive" and, after all, "the mind is what counts" (notice how often characters in this play talk like advertisements); an aspirin will "soothe" him. Willy stops short of admitting that he almost hit a kid (he will tell Happy that later), but he does reach out one more time to Linda when he says, "I have such thoughts. I have such strange thoughts." Instead of responding to his plea for understanding, Linda takes refuge in a practical solution: a job in New York will solve Willy's problems.

Actually, a job in New York, even supposing for a moment that Willy could get one, would not cure the widening fissure in Willy Loman's psyche, his looming nervous breakdown. Immediately, the audience sees both the reason for Linda's support of her husband (her fierce, protective love for him) and the inherent danger of her feeding his illusions. Why Linda acts as she does, and the degree to which her reaction makes her complicit in Willy's death, is a question to bear in mind. Miller gave his own answer in his commentary for the Beijing production of the play:

> Linda sustains the illusion because that's the only way Willy can be sustained. At the same time any cure or change is impossible in Willy. Ironically, she's helping to guarantee that Willy will never recover from his illusion. She has to support it; she has no alternative, given his nature and hers.

Clues to what is actually wrong with Willy come when he describes driving the car before he found himself losing control. He is surprised to recall that he was "looking at scenery" because being on the road every day has made him numb to the beauties of New England. In his mind, he was back over a decade in his 1928 Chevy which had an opening windshield. Here, then, is the opposition between the life of the salesman that he *actually* lives and the life in the outdoors that part of him *wishes* to live: here is the opposition between the natural and the urban world in which he is trapped. Ironically, getting a job in New York would cut him off even further from the outdoors which an essential part of him (a repressed part to be sure) loves.

Willy has been trapped by his job in just the same way that his house has been trapped by the encroaching city – a gradual but inexorable process. He remembers the semi-rural nature of Brooklyn when they first moved in, and the two "beautiful elm trees out there" – long since cut down. Their house has come to represent the constriction of Willy's hopes, ironically even as his twenty-five years of mortgage payments is nearly complete. Urban development to accommodate more people has stifled the neighborhood, "The street is lined with cars. There's not a breath of fresh air ... The grass don't grow ... you can't raise a carrot..." Although he is not aware of it, Willy is here describing the barrenness of his own "*Lost*" soul. When he later tells Linda, "some people – some people accomplish something," he is implicitly accepting that he is not one of these people, much as he has aspired to their dream.

Against such honesty, we must place Willy's dishonesty. Rather than admitting defeat, he clings to his commercial identity as "the New England man ... vital in New England," and resolves to reschedule his appointment with Brown and Morrison convincing himself that he "could sell them!" Yet it is clear that his triumphs (such as they were) are not only in the past, but that they exist more in Willy's mind than they *ever* did in reality. Thus, he remembers old man Wagner as "a prince ... a masterful man" who, unlike his son Howard, appreciated Willy, and boasts that when he first went north "the Wagner company didn't know where New England was!" – a claim that associates his own achievement with that of the pioneers of the Frontier like his father and elder brother. (As the play progresses, we will learn not to believe Willy's versions of the past.)

Willy desperately clings to his own distorted vision of his past and his present because acknowledging the truth would shatter the illusion that he is fulfilling his dream; it would destroy him. This is why he is so sensitive whenever someone disagrees with him. He is tired of "always being contradicted." This explains his anger when Linda tells him she has bought a different kind of cheese. Willy does not want change because change disrupts his fragile belief that he is in control of his life.

The greatest challenge to Willy's image of himself is his elder son Biff because Biff has not achieved the success in business for which Willy prepared him. This means that one of two things must be true: either the dreams, values and skills which Willy inculcated into his son were wrong, or Biff is entirely responsible for his own failure. This is why Willy must blame Biff, calling him "a lazy bum" who is wasting his life working on a farm in Texas when he should be making a career in the city. We see here a clash between the American Dream of the nineteenth century which involved heading out into the wilds of the frontier (as Willy's father and older brother Ben did, and as Willy himself sometimes wishes he had done), and the American Dream of the twentieth century which involves making a financial success in the city.

Willy must insist that America is "the greatest country in the world," and that Biff is responsible for his own failure because this allows him to evade Linda's criticism of his latest outburst against Biff's lack of material success. Instead of trying to understand his son, Willy perseveres with the dream of getting "him a job in selling" where, "He could be big in no time" – it is the same old dream Willy has always clung onto, that a man with personality and pep can make it to the top. This leads Willy into inevitable contradiction, for to succeed Biff must be "not lazy" but rather a "hard worker," a person with the capacity to fulfill his father's expectations of him. Increasingly, Willy disappears from the problematic present into 'memories' of how things were when Biff was in high school, a talented athlete, adored by his peers, and seeing Willy as a hero – a time when things were hopeful. The SparkNotes editors make the point very well when they write, "Willy changes his interpretation of reality according to his psychological needs at the moment."

Typically, Linda tries to restore the relationship between father and son. She defends Biff telling Willy that he is still "finding himself." She knows that Biff is "still lost ... very lost," but as with her husband, she makes no effort to examine the problem. To some extent, Linda also escapes into the past. The return of her two sons allows her to recapture the image of them as teenagers, when the house was peaceful and hopeful, "It was so nice to see them shaving together, one behind the other." She regrets the division into which her family has fallen, but she makes no serious attempt to understand it; she simply tries to paper over the cracks in the relationship between Willy and his two sons. (Although the emphasis in the play is always on the antagonism between Willy and Biff, it becomes clear later that Happy's relationship with his father is also fractured and dysfunctional.)

There is one more moment of honesty from Willy when he asks Linda, "You're not worried about me, are you, sweetheart?" We later discover that Linda is worried sick that her husband will commit suicide, but she says nothing, except to offer vague reassurance. Willy tells her, "You're my foundation and my support." There is tragic irony in this, for by supporting him in the way that she does, Linda simply makes inevitable his eventual crack-up.

Real Time Dialogue between Biff and Happy ("Happy: Jesus, maybe he smashed..." to "Happy: Sh ... Sleep, Biff.")

17. Contrast the explanations that Happy and Biff give for Willy's problems with driving. Which is closer to the truth?
18. In what ways are Happy and Biff shown also to be living in the past?
19. How does Happy try to explain the tension that he knows exists between Biff and their father? How does Biff react to Happy's explanation?
20. Biff describes how he has lived since failing to graduate from high school. He has actually lived two very different kinds of life. What are they? What are the pros and cons to him of each of these different ways of life?
21. Why does Happy call Biff "a poet ... an idealist!"?
22. In contrast to Biff, Happy has led only one kind if life since high school. List the aspects of his current way of life that trouble Happy and prevent him from being contented.
23. Biff suggests that the solution to his own discontent and that of his brother

is for them to go out West together, "maybe ... buy a ranch." How does Biff feel that this arrangement would solve his own discontent? Although he is said to be *"enthralled"* by Biff's idea, Happy rejects it. Explain why.

24. Biff explains that he is planning to ask his former employer, Bill Oliver, for a loan of "seven or eight thousand dollars." Immediately, Biff and Happy have a difference of opinion about what Biff should use that money for. Explain why Happy wants Biff to "come back here" and work for Oliver again, and why that is the last thing Biff wants to do.

25. How does the text make it perfectly clear that Oliver is *never* going to give Biff either a job or a loan?

26. During the dialogue between Biff and Happy, Willy's voice is heard occasionally. What can we conclude about Willy's mental state from the things that we hear him say?

Notes

The end of the scene presents the director and stage designer with a logistical problem: Happy and Biff are seen by the audience upstairs in their beds, but in a very short space of time must reappear (as their younger selves) on the front of the stage. Young Happy and Young Biff are (to the best of my knowledge) always played by the same actors who play their older selves, and certainly this was Miller's intention since it points to the continuity (one might rather say the concurrence) of past and present in Willy's mind. (Read Jo Mielziner's account of how he solved this problem in the stage design for the first production, in an essay which is included in Gerald Weales's edition of the play, pages 187-198.)

Commentary

Biff and Happy are back in the bedroom (significantly called *"the boys' room"* in the stage directions) that they shared up to the moment Biff left home fifteen years ago. This alerts the audience to the fact that, in many ways, both men seem to be trapped in perpetual adolescence. Now in their early- and mid-thirties, neither man has put down roots: neither is married, and neither has the sort of job that will bring in enough money for them to think of themselves as successful. On this evening, both are living in the past: Happy reminisces about, "All the talk that went across those two beds, huh? Our whole lives," and about his first sexual experience, and Biff reminds him that he arranged it for him. Even the names "Happy" and "Biff" are childlike, inappropriate for mature adults. (In the restaurant scene in Act Two, Happy will introduce himself to the young woman as "Harold" and claim that "Happy" is his nickname.)

Miller clearly differentiates the brothers when he writes that Happy *"like his brother, is lost, but in a different way, for he has never allowed himself to turn his face toward defeat and is thus more confused and hard-skinned, although seemingly more content."* Happy has espoused Willy's dream of

11

success in sales, and although he was always less favored by his father than Biff, he seems to be emulating the qualities that Willy encouraged in his elder brother: personality, aggressive sexuality and willingness to bend the rules. However, despite following his father's advice and his brother's example, Happy has not achieved success in selling, although he does make enough to afford to rent an apartment, to own a car, and to date lots of women (and have lots of sex). None of this, however, brings him contentment because his desire for success, and the power that comes with it, is thwarted by the reality of his lowly position in the firm. To compensate for his failure, Happy seeks to gain power over women. He refers to the first girl he ever had sex with as "a pig!" and his euphemism for seduction, "knockin' them over," suggests more than a failure to respect the women he seduces: it suggests a violence. He targets women who are in relationships with his superiors and "ruins" them in order to prove to himself that he can get one over on the men above him on the corporate ladder. In his mind, this compensates for having to work for men who are, he feels, inferior to himself in terms of their physical development and skills. He boasts to Biff, "I can outbox, outrun, and outlift anybody in that store, and I have to take orders from those common, petty sons-of-bitches..." This is an immature basis for comparison.

Biff also lacks self-knowledge, but unlike Happy, he is pulled apart by contradictory desires. We are told "*his dreams are stronger and less acceptable than Happy's*," but what this does not tell us is that his dreams are an *alternative* to Willy's and Happy's dream of being successful through selling. Biff enjoys working outside on a farm, but when spring comes around, he becomes impatient and feels the need to return to New York and "make something of himself" – the goal that Willy has laid down. Biff's instability explains his inability to maintain a steady job – he is always on the move, drifting from one unfulfilling job to the next. He also has conflicting emotions for his father. Part of him loves Willy, and he is genuinely horrified by Happy's report of Willy talking to himself. On the other hand, Biff resents Willy's antagonism toward him and vehemently denies any responsibility for his father's condition, without ever being able to tell his mother and brother the real cause of his alienation from Willy. All he can do is hint that Willy is troubled because of "other things" besides the fact that he (Biff) is working as a farmhand, a job that Willy despises as unmanly. At times, however, Biff feels just the same way about himself: he feels that he is just a boy and must do something to shift into the maturity of adulthood. The truth is that Biff is driven by *conflicting* desires: he wants to please his father (a desire that he denies and hides from himself) and to call him out as a fake (a desire that he knows he cannot fulfill without destroying both Willy and Linda).

At the start of the scene, Biff makes the same kind of excuses for Willy's driving problems as did Linda earlier, suggesting that his eye-sight is going or that he is color-blind. Just like his mother, Biff tries to avoid confronting the true scale and cause of Willy's problems, although in Biff's case there is an element of self-preservation in his evasion. Happy does not understand what happened to his brother's "old humor, the old confidence," but Biff deflects his questions while denying responsibility for his father's problems. When Biff is finally very honest with Happy, telling him, "I don't know – what I'm supposed to want," Happy is incapable of understanding him. In order to explain, Biff describes in detail the contrast between working nine-to-five for fifty weeks a year in business and the freedom and beauty of working on a ranch. Happy is able to recognize, but not to *empathize with*, his experience, "You're a poet, you know that, Biff. You're a – you're an idealist!" Happy, by contrast, is a pragmatist.

Biff wants Happy to join him in Texas. Both of the boys have difficulty dealing with authority, and Biff is right when he tells Happy, "we weren't brought up to grub for money. I don't know how to do it." Biff believes owning their own business in the form of a ranch would be the ideal way of life for both of them to reconcile the competing dreams that motivate them. Biff's problem, as at times he is fully aware, is that he still accepts his father's definition of success as getting on in business, getting married, having children and building a future. Whilst both incompatible dreams coexist in his psyche, Biff will never be contented in life.

As Happy outlines his business life, we learn that he is not "content" because promotion depends upon waiting "for the merchandise manager to die" – success does not come as rapidly as Willy had led his boys to expect. More fundamentally, Happy has seen that so-called success, while it brings material possessions, does not satisfy the soul. When Biff proposes that the two go out West, Happy is initially enthusiastic because the vision of physical work appeals to something deep inside him; however, he is pulled back by his father's dream. He has been taught to want "the waves [to] part in front of him" when he walks into a store; he needs to prove that he can "make the grade." Happy admits that his "overdeveloped sense of competition" leads him to seduce the women of men who are his business associates and to take bribes. Happy's problem is that he does not understand the true nature of the frustration that explains his acting in this way: the two sides of his personality explain his contradictions, "I hate myself for it. Because I don't want the girl, and, still, I take it and – I love it!"

Happy attempts to establish order in his life by proposing that Biff come back to the city and use his contacts to get a start in business; Biff, however, wants to buy a ranch so that he can "do the work I like and still be something." We can see him here desperately trying to reconcile two mutually exclusive life-styles. There is another problem: Biff's plan depends upon a former employer being willing to lend him between seven and ten thousand dollars to buy a ranch – the same employer who was about to fire Biff because he had stolen "that carton of basketballs." This dialogue has established for the audience the nature of the problems that the young men have and the sad fact that each is trying to solve his problems through different forms of self-deception and denial.

Willy's First Imaginative Recreation of the Past ("Willy: Just wanna be careful…" to "Willy: He's got spirit, personality…")

27. Explain the contradictory nature of Willy's comments on Biff's relationship with girls.
28. Before Biff and Happy actually enter to join Willy, what indications are given that all three characters are good at working with their hands and that they enjoy doing so?
29. Why does Happy suddenly say, "I'm losing weight, you notice, Pop?"? [It is a line he will repeat several times throughout the play.]
30. Explain the contradictory nature of Willy's reaction when he realizes that Biff has "borrowed" the football. Explain the fallacy in Willy's belief that, because Biff is likable, "Coach'll probably congratulate" him on his "initiative."
31. Explain the difference, in Willy's mind, between being "liked" and being "well-liked."
32. Willy boasts that, "America is full of beautiful towns and fine, upstanding people. And they know me, boys, they know me up and down New England." Evaluate the actual evidence in Willy's account of his recent trip that he uses to support this claim.
33. Biff describes a special play he is going to make for Willy during Saturday's game. What does this show about the influence Willy has had on his son's decision-making? What is significant about Happy's reaction?
34. Explain why Willy is so scornful of Bernard.
35. The following represents Willy's credo, "the man who makes an appearance in the business world, the man who creates personal interest, is the man who gets ahead." This is the core of Willy's guidance to his sons. Explain how it inevitably sets both of them up for frustration and failure.
36. The part of the scene in which Biff's friends wait in the basement not knowing "what to do with themselves," where they instantly "sweep out the furnace room" when he tells them to, and where George, Sam and Frank happily hang out Linda's washing for the same reason, is frequently criticized as being unrealistic. Actually, Miller deliberately writes it so that it *is* unbelievable. Explain why.
37. The first signs that Willy's idyllic reconstruction of a successful and promising past is beginning to disintegrate occur in his dialogue with Linda. What are they?

38. Why do the Loman's owe "a hundred and twenty dollars"? What is Willy's reaction to his failure to earn enough money to pay these outstanding bills?
39. Contrast what Willy tells Linda about the way he is received by buyers with the earlier account that he gave his sons. Account for the difference.
40. How does Linda react to Willy's expression of self-doubt about the way he is perceived by others?
41. What triggers in Willy's mind the brief scene between him and The Woman? [Comment on the pun on the word "make."]
42. Why is Willy attracted to The Woman? [Remember that everything she says is the product of Willy's mind rather than a record of what might actually have happened.]
43. When Willy says, "I'll make it all up to you, Linda...," to what is he referring? Comment on the importance of the word "all."
44. Why does Willy get so annoyed when he sees his wife mending her stockings?
45. Willy's idyll crashes suddenly into nightmare. Explain precisely *how* this happens.
46. What do you think that Mr. Birnbaum means by calling Biff "stuck up"?
47. Explain why this 'memory' scene ends where it does.

Notes

"It's got Gene Tunney's signature on it!": James Joseph ('Gene') Tunney (1897-1978) held the world heavyweight boxing title from 1926 to 1928 when he retired as undefeated champion. In fact, he fought eighty-five times and lost only once. Celebrity product endorsement is a common marketing tool, and it is interesting the Willy, a salesman, falls for it.

"Two hundred gross ... Makes seventy dollars and some pennies": I have never seen this pointed out elsewhere, but it seems that Linda is calculating Willy's earnings on a commission basis, yet at this time in his career Willy was on a salary. On a salary, his earnings would *not* depend upon how much he sold (unless he had a separate bonus for sales, but that is not what Linda says). The only explanation I can think of is that Willy is projecting back his currents status as a salesman working on commission, which would make sense since the memory sequences are informed by his mind's knowledge of what will subsequently happen to each of the people involved.

Commentary

What we see on stage now is *not* a flashback – flashbacks in drama or novels are reliable portrayals of what happened in the past. The scene presented here is the first of several that are happening *in real time* in the present. They are happening, however, inside Willy's head, this one while he sits in the kitchen drinking a glass of milk. (Miller's original title for the play was *In His Head.*) These scenes do not occur at random; each memory is triggered by something that happens in the real-time action and Willy is changed by what he experiences. Willy is reliving the past *not* as it was but as he now *needs to remember it* to have been. However, as Dr. Daniel Schneider points out, Willy is not in control of what his mind creates:

> The past, as in hallucination, comes back to him; not chronologically as in a flashback. But dynamically with the inner logic of his erupting volcanic unconscious. In psychiatry we call this "the return of the repressed," when a mind breaks under the invasion of primitive impulses no longer capable of compromise with reality. ("Play of Dreams," Weales ed. 252)

Willy's reconstruction of his relationship with his two sons during their high school years begins as an idyll: a lighting change fades out the oppressive apartment houses and "*the entire house and surroundings become covered with leaves.*" This reflects the change that has happened to the once semi-rural neighborhood over the last fifteen or so years, but the return of flute music indicates that the change also evokes much deeper associations with the frontier past of the country and the values that the frontier demanded.

It is 1932: Biff is seventeen and Happy fifteen. On the surface, Willy emerges as the patriarch of the family, a successful salesman, idolized by both of his sons, whose success in life (Biff's in particular) is assured by the excellent advice and preparation they are receiving from their father. As the recollection continues, however, Willy cannot prevent the part of his mind that knows the truth from undermining this idyllic picture with details that indicate the reality behind the façade. Willy's first speech shows the unacknowledged contradiction in his mind between Biff watching his "schooling first" and the importance of "makin' a hit" – as always, it is the latter that wins out.

The skill with which the boys simonize the car, and the pleasure that Willy takes in their work, indicates their shared love of manual work, as does Willy's anticipation of taking down the tree branch to prevent it from falling on the house. This is something that he knows how to do. Here Willy gives his son's good advice, "Never leave a job till you're finished – remember that." The gift of the punching bag likewise derives from Willy's love of physicality, but it also speaks to his desire for winning which is again evident when he laughs about Biff's "initiative" in taking the football from the locker room – he is teaching Biff that being a winner involves being prepared to break the rules, because the rules apply only to losers. It is the difference between being "liked" and being "well liked" that separates the two. Willy's account of his recent trip to New England aims to show his boys that the "finest people" know him, but the only evidence he provides is that he met the Mayor of Providence in a hotel lobby and bought him coffee.

Speaking of the up-coming game, Biff promises to "break through for a touchdown" just for Willy. Perhaps with more than a hint of jealousy (one of several indications in this scene that Happy feels resentful at being overlooked by his father), Happy reminds his brother that he's "supposed to pass," but Willy is delighted by the idea – another illustration of his belief that exceptional individuals are above the rules. This continues when he mocks the studious Bernard, who reminds Biff that he should be studying (the very same thing Willy himself said at the start of this scene), dismissing him as a "pest" and an "anemic." Willy is impressed with Biff's "beautiful job of printing" 'University of Virginia' on his sneakers (just as he was impressed by Gene Tunney's signature printed on the punching bag), but Bernard takes the realistic view that printing UV on his sneakers "doesn't mean they've got to graduate him." When Bernard leaves, Willy voices his credo: in business, personality is more important that education; appearance is more important than substance.

The idea that there is a "cellar full of boys ... [who] don't know what to do with themselves" without Biff's leadership, that they happily sweep out the furnace room on his say so, that Sam and George rush to hang out the washing (and, we may add, the earlier detail that the girls pay for Biff) have frequently been criticized as unconvincing. However, this misses the point that they only happen in Willy's head: his memory distorts the past to exaggerate Biff's preeminence.

At this point, the idyll (which has always contained ominous undertones like the threat of Biff not graduating) begins to fall apart. It is clear that even in 'the good old days,' Willy "suffered ... from mood swings and an almost unconscious and certainly bazaar habit of self-contradiction ... [Evidently he had] a highly unstable and vulnerable personality" (Bloom ed. *Guides* 35). Though he has boasted that on his trip he, "Knocked 'em cold in Providence, slaughtered 'em in Boston," and now tells Linda that he "was sellin' thousands and thousands," the truth is that he made just over $70 on the trip. Of course, he makes excuses: he was selling well but just had to come home, and "three of the stores were half closed for inventory in Boston." The ever-practical Linda calculates that their bills come to around $120. In another evasion, Willy blames the appliances they have bought: the refrigerator (which had "the biggest adds of any of them!"), the roof repair, the washing machine and the vacuum cleaner (perhaps bought on the installment plan), and the car (Willy, who has just said "Chevrolet, Linda, is the greatest car ever built," now shouts, "That goddam Chevrolet, they ought to prohibit the manufacture of that car!"). Willy must either blame himself for failing to earn enough to maintain a middle class lifestyle, or he must blame the system (the poor quality of the appliances, the high cost of repairs, and the installment plan payments), so he blames the system.

Suddenly, Willy is deeply honest, telling his wife, "the trouble is ... people don't seem to take to me ... They seem to laugh at me ...they pass me by ... I'm fat, I'm very – foolish to look at ... they do laugh at me. I know that." This amounts to an admission not of the false nature of his dream (for he sees other men being successful), but of his personal failure. Linda reassures him because she loves him: he is "making seventy to a hundred dollars a week"; he is "lively" by nature; he is "the handsomest man in the world" to her. Linda's support brings on Willy's guilt at having been unfaithful to her. (This is clear to the audience because "*The Woman, dimly seen, is dressing.*") He comes close to admitting his guilt when he tells Linda "I get so lonely – especially when business is bad and there's nobody to talk to."

At this point, however, Willy's mind needs to remember (or rather construct) a moment of triumph. The transition to the scene with The Woman is made by a pun on the word 'make': when Willy says "There's so much I want to make for –" he is referring to his deep need to "make a living for [Linda], or a business, a business for the boys," but The Woman interprets the word in its colloquial sense of 'picked up.' It flatters Willy's ego that his mistress chooses him because she thinks he is "a wonderful man" and she laughs at his jokes. The Woman obviously existed, but how much of this dialogue actually happened is open to question. The detail of the gifts of stockings that Willy gives her hints that he is, in effect, paying The Woman for sex with luxury gifts. The 'memory' does, however, make Willy feel even more guilty because his mistress has the stockings that ought to be Linda's. It also provides context for the way in which Biff and Happy treat girls and young women as sex objects to be used and discarded. In Biff, this might be related to him having discovered his father's unfaithfulness, but in both it springs fundamentally from Willy's constant demeaning of Linda.

At this point, Willy's idyll turns into a nightmare: his guilt makes him explode at Linda for mending her stockings; Bernard predicts Biff's failure in the Regents; Linda complains that Biff is "too rough with the girls"; and Biff is driving without a license. Initially, Willy blames Biff saying, "I'll whip him!" but then he falls back on denial trying to blank out the warning signs, and when Linda hints that Willy is teaching his son the wrong values, he asserts, "There's nothing the matter with him! You want him to be a worm like Bernard! He's got spirit, personality…" It is a desperate attempt to convince *himself* that he raised Biff with the right values and the right dream. At this point the 'memory' fades. Beginning as a recollection of how wonderful life was when the boys were in high school, it has degenerated into a display of the reasons for the failures to come: Willy's own inadequacy and lies and Biff's faulty values. The fact that Linda exits "*almost in tears*" indicates how helpless she feels to correct the mistakes that she sees Willy making.

Return to Real Time ("Willy: Loaded with it." to "Charley: Don't call me disgusting, Willy.")

48. Willy says, "I never in my life taught him anything but decent things."

Based on the evidence of the play so far, how true is this assertion?
49. How relevant is Ben's success in the "jungle" at the end of the nineteenth century to achieving success in the business world in the mid-twentieth century?
50. For a moment, with Happy, Willy is totally honest about his situation (as he was with Linda when he first came home earlier in the evening and with Happy when he described the near-accident he had in Yonkers). Explain what he means when he says, "Where are you guys, where are you?" and, "The woods are burning" (which is, on the face of it, a strange metaphor for Willy to use to describe the failure of his career).
51. How does Willy attempt to establish his superiority over Charley? Why is it so important to Willy that he does this?
52. Why does Charley offer Willy a job? And while we are on this topic, *how* does Charley offer Willy a job? Why does Willy refuse the offer?
53. This short dialogue shows the different attitudes that Willy and Charley have to parenting. Explain the difference. What is Charley trying to tell Willy when he says, "When a deposit bottle is broken you don't get your nickel back"?
54. How does Charley attempt to bolster Willy's self-esteem? How does his effort backfire into an argument?

Notes

"When a deposit bottle is broken you don't get your nickel back": Before plastics, all bottles were glass. Some glass bottles had a returnable nickel deposit to encourage people to recycle them.

Commentary

Willy begins with self-justification, trying to convince himself that "I never in my life told him [Biff] anything but decent things" – a claim we have just seen to be untrue. He blames Linda for waxing the floors, but the truth is that she does it because she cannot afford to employ someone else to do it – a tangible reminder of Willy's failure as a provider. (In Act Two, we will learn that Willy's boss, Howard, employs a maid.) Willy is, however, remarkably honest in admitting to Happy that he, "Nearly hit a kid in Yonkers." His is a mind at the end of its tether.

Whenever he feels overwhelmed by his lack of success, as he does now, Willy re-calls his brother Ben's proposition and regrets that he did not accept it: if only he had gone to work for Ben in Alaska, he would be rich now. Ben symbolizes Willy's idealized version of the pure American Dream: he was an adventurer who walked into the wild and came out rich because, "The man knew what he wanted and went out and got it!" However, Willy still believes in a *different* version of the dream, applying Ben's qualities and values to the world of business and becoming a successful salesman. Thus, he blames

Happy's failure on his personal weakness, telling his son, "The world is an oyster, but you don't crack it open on a mattress!" (a reference to Happy's womanizing). Willy mocks his son's promise to fund his retirement while earning only "seventy goddam dollars a week" (ironically the same sum that he himself made on his sales trip in the last scene).

Again, Willy is frighteningly honest, telling Happy (and more importantly himself), "I couldn't get past Yonkers today! Where are you guys, where are you? The woods are burning! I can't drive a car!" The disconnected nature of these statements reflects Willy's fragmenting psyche. He realizes that his sons are not there for him, but for this he blames their faults rather than acknowledging his own. More fundamentally, he realizes that America is no longer for him the land of opportunity (symbolized by the woods) that it once was.

Charley comes over because he is concerned about his friend; like Linda, he has probably experienced Willy coming home unexpectedly before. The audience already knows that Willy is jealous of Charley because of his success – remember that Willy's boast that he would one day own a business bigger than Charley's has come to nothing. Though he does it with the best of intentions, inevitably, by offering him a job, Charley reminds Willy of his failure. To the man who is lending him fifty dollars a week to make up his salary, Willy rather absurdly boasts that he has "got a job." To make himself feel superior, Willy belittles Charley's ignorance of vitamins and his ineptness with tools. Willy says, "A man who can't handle tools is not a man. You're disgusting." Even the usually mild-mannered Charley is angered by this attack on his manhood; he knows what motivates Willy to lash out, but this does not make it any less painful when he does so.

As with Linda and Happy, however, there are moments when Willy lets the mask drop and is frighteningly honest with Charley. He admits, "I can't understand it. [Biff's] going back to Texas again. What the hell is that? ... I got nothing to give him, Charley, I'm clean, I'm clean." Charley gives his friend the best advice anyone gives him in the play: let Biff go to Texas because he won't starve. He uses a metaphor, "When a deposit bottle is broken you don't get your nickel back." He is actually advising Willy to give up on his dreams, but that is something he will never do.

Willy's Second Imaginative Recreation of the Past ("Willy: I'm getting awfully..." to "Willy: I was right!")

55. The transition to Willy's memory of Ben's first visit to Brooklyn is gradual. Explain Charley's confusion during this transition.
56. What personal qualities enabled Ben to become rich? How applicable are those qualities to Willy's situation in the modern business world?
57. According to Ben, what qualities and skills enabled their father to become

rich? How applicable are those qualities and skills to Willy's situation?

58. What is Ben's attitude to competition? How does Linda react to the lesson in boxing that Ben gives Biff?

59. How does Willy attempt to convince his brother that there is continuity between the world in which Ben and their father (supposedly) prospered and the world that Willy now inhabits? How convincing do you find Willy's argument?

60. Comment on the different reactions of Ben and Charley to the stealing that Willy encourages Biff and Happy to do.

61. Why does Willy so desperately need from Ben validation of his own life and his parenting of his two boys? What exactly does Ben say that convinces Willy that he has been right? Right about what?

Commentary

This time, past and present coexist in Willy's mind, and he is incapable of distinguishing them. To Willy, Ben is just as real as is Charley, who has no idea that Willy is seeing and hearing Ben. It is not surprising that Charley becomes confused during the card game. Willy, however, becomes "*unnerved*" when he realizes that he is hallucinating and picks a quarrel with Charley in order to get rid of him.

To Willy, Ben is "the only man I ever met who knew the answers." Willy has derived his understanding of the personal qualities necessary for success directly from his rather incomplete knowledge of Ben, the only self-made man he has ever known. (In Willy's mind, Ben began much poorer than Charley and ended up, in less than five years, very much richer.) This is, however, a grave mistake since Willy's psychology is much more complex than that of Ben, for whom life is very simple, "Why, boys, when I was seventeen I walked into the jungle, and when I was twenty-one I walked out ... And by God I was rich." That is really as much as we ever learn about *how* Ben made his fortune (because it is as much as Willy knows); not only is it pretty unspecific, but it is hard to see how it is applicable to the life of a salesman working in twentieth century New England. Judging himself against the criterion of his father's and his brother's largely mythical financial success, Willy *must always* count himself as a failure. There is no 'average' for Willy, only success and failure – which is unfortunate since Willy is a very average salesman, neither great nor terrible at his job.

In this scene, we learn more about Willy's background. Ben tells us that their father was an artisan craftsman who travelled across the country in a wagon with his family selling "the flutes that he'd made on the way." Ben also says, much less probably, that he was a "Great inventor ...With one gadget he made more than a man like you could make in a lifetime." Nothing in the rest of Ben's narrative supports this idea. In fact, their father ran out on the family to go to Alaska, and Ben abandoned the three-years- and-eleven-months-old Willy under a wagon in South Dakota to follow him. Willy's entire life can be seen as a hopeless attempt to rebuild the pieces of the broken, fatherless family of his childhood. This is why it is so important to Willy to have the approval of his professional contacts (to be "well liked'), why he desperately wants to be a good father and provider, and why he must leave his sons a material inheritance, for his own father did none of these things.

In so far as we learn anything about the secret of Ben's success, it is that by pure chance he was in the right place at the right time and that in that situation he was completely ruthless. Having 'illegally' tripped Biff in their sparring match, he opines, "Never fight fair with a stranger, boy. You'll never get out of the jungle that way." Willy completely lacks that degree of ruthlessness, though he is desperate to convince Ben (and himself) that he is as "wild-hearted" as was his father and as prepared to break the rules as was Ben. Thus, he describes hunting in Brooklyn and sends his boys off to steal sand. Ben, the voice of the nineteenth century frontier, totally approves, but Charley, the voice of twentieth century urban life, warns of the consequences, and these force their way into Willy's mind as his daydream turns into a nightmare of the watchman chasing Biff. Although he never rationalizes this, Willy equates modern capitalism with the colonial jungle: those who succeed do so because they do not let morality stand in their way (Ben counters Charley's assertion that "the jails are full of fearless characters" with the counter-assertion, "And the stock exchange, friend!"). In doing so, Willy ignores the virtues of education, hard work and self-discipline as exemplified by Charley and Bernard.

As Ben readies himself to leave, Willy again comes close to honesty. He admits that "Business is bad, it's murderous," but then adds defensively, "But not for me, of course." He boasts of his "fine position here," but admits to feeling "kind of temporary about [himself]," though he clearly does not understand why. He admits that sometimes he is afraid that he is not teaching Biff and Happy "the right kind of –." It is significant that Willy cannot even find the words to complete that thought. Willy worries that he has taught his sons (particularly Biff) to consider themselves exceptionally gifted and therefore destined to succeed no matter how hard they work (or do not work). What Willy needs is validation, and in his hallucination Ben gives it, though the audience is aware that all Ben does is repeat his credo about the jungle. Ben then abandons Willy yet again because he has investments in Alaska to look into. Nevertheless, the 'memory' has served its psychological purpose.

Return to Real Time ("Linda: Willy, dear? Willy?" to "Biff: A carpenter is allowed to whistle!")

62. Explain the significance of Willy having pawned Ben's "diamond watch fob" to pay for "Biff's radio correspondence course." [NB. Look at the

chronology into which Biff's course fits.]

63. The dialogue between Linda and her sons (particularly Biff) gives us more insight than we have previously had into her situation and how she is attempting to deal with it. What evidence does Linda give of her resentment against Happy and Biff for how they have treated their father? What ultimatum does Linda give Biff? Why?

64. Explain why Biff tells his mother, "He always, wiped the floor with you. Never had an ounce of respect for you," and why Happy rushes to Willy's defense.

65. How does Linda justify her passionate belief that "attention must be paid" to Willy, that "He's not to be allowed to fall into his grave like an old dog"?

66. What shocking facts about Willy's financial situation do Happy and Biff learn for the first time from Linda? How does each of them react?

67. Examine Linda's explanation for Willy's falling productivity in sales for the company ("Are they any worse ... philandering bum –"). How honest is she being here?

68. What shocking facts about Willy's mental condition do Happy and Biff learn from Linda? How do they react?

69. Explain *why* Biff compulsively whistled "whole songs in the elevator like a clown" when he worked for Bob Harrison. What other fault does Happy find with the way Biff conducted himself when working for Harrison?

70. Happy says, "I'll tell you something that I hate to say, Biff, but in the business world some of them think you're crazy." Do you think he really hates to say that, or that he really enjoys saying it? Explain your answer. Explain how the argument that this remark initiates shows the vast difference between Happy and his brother. How close does Biff come to realizing the truth about himself?

Commentary

In his yard, Willy looks up at the sky, commenting to Linda, "Gotta break your neck to see a star in this yard." This is an effective image of the way in which Willy's love of the great outdoors, which he inherited from his father, has been stifled and restricted as a result of the choice he made to seek success in selling (i.e., in the city) and by his rejection of Ben's offer of a job in Alaska. His enquiry about the "watch fob with a diamond in it" that Ben gave him represents Willy's desire to connect himself with his brother's success. However, the fact that he pawned the watch to pay for "Biff's radio correspondence course" shows how he has invested (and lost) everything he had in a failed dream – he has pawned the ideal of the frontier adventurer for the job of traveling salesman.

Linda gets angry with Biff and Happy because both have abandoned her to look after Willy alone, and now seem to be shocked by his condition. She calls Happy "a philandering bum," showing that she is fully aware that he has neither real ambition nor real love for his father, whose example he is now following. The problem Linda has with Biff is that she does not know the cause of Biff's alienation from his father; she does not understand why Willy threw Biff out of the house. As a result, she too blames him for his failure to grow up. When he tells her, "I can't get hold of some form of life," she is unsympathetic, asserting, "Biff, a man is not a bird, to come and go with the springtime." This could have been said by Willy – except that he lacks Linda's poetic expression. Because she does not know the origin of the constant arguments between Biff and Willy, she takes her husband's side and gives Biff an ultimatum, "Either he's your father and you pay him that respect, or else you're not to come here." Both Linda and Happy are shocked when Biff tells his mother, "Stop making excuses for him! He always, always wiped the floor with you. Never once had an ounce of respect for you." Without knowing it, Linda almost goads Biff into revealing the truth, "I know he's a fake and he doesn't like anybody around who knows." This means nothing to Linda, and Biff refuses to explain when she asks, "What do you mean?" As a result, nothing is resolved.

Linda sees the truth about Willy's economic and psychological situation and she succeeds in conveying to her sons that matters have reached a crisis. She tells them that Willy has been on commission for the last five weeks; that he is borrowing money from Charley and lying to her about it; that he has tried to kill himself by crashing the car; and that he is preparing to gas himself. Shocked by these revelations, Biff promises to apply himself, "It's just – you see, Mom, I don't fit in business. Not that I won't try. I'll try, and I'll make good." This is self-contradictory and self-defeating nonsense: the first part is spoken by the part of Biff that loves the outdoors and the second part is simply repeating the credo that Willy has drummed into him – a credo that he knows to be phony.

This is made clear by the quarrel between Happy and Biff that ends this scene. Happy (again motivated subconsciously by jealousy) criticizes his brother for "whistling whole songs in the elevator" (an inherent habit than he shares with Willy and which links both of them with the flute music that Biff's grandfather made) and going off to swim when he should be working without covering himself. The argument is between one brother who has bought into his father's dream (despite the fact that it has made him miserably dissatisfied with his life) and the other who has seen through that dream (though he has not yet emancipated himself from its hold or espoused an alternative). It does, however, force Biff to a moment of epiphany when he is able to put into words exactly why he will never follow Willy's dream, "Screw the business world ... we don't belong in this nuthouse of a city! We should be mixing cement on some open plain, or – or carpenters. A carpenter can whistle!" At this stage in the play, however, Willy's mental condition means that doing what he "should" be doing is not an option for Biff.

Linda's priority is to keep Willy working by doing so keep him alive, and in order to do this she must bolster his faith in himself. Thus, she conspires to maintain his illusions: Linda must deny in her words and actions the truths that she knows. She does this because of her unqualified love for Willy which leads her to protect him from the crushing reality of his situation, from the insensitivity and indifference of his two sons, and ultimately from his own despair. The struggle has taken its toll on Linda who, though not yet sixty, is looking old – a fact that shocks Biff.

Miller uses the character of Linda to present Willy as a man worthy of respect despite his lowly social position and the many faults in his character. In three key speeches, Linda speaks poetically of Willy's fall, "he's a human being, and a terrible thing is happening to him. So attention must be paid ... The man is exhausted ... A small man can be just as exhausted as a great man." Ostensibly, Linda is talking to Happy and Biff, but her true audience is anyone who sees the play. Her feelings about the dignity of the play's protagonist are shared by Miller.

Continuation in Real Time ("Willy: Even your grandfather..." to "Willy: ... between the buildings!")

71. Why does Willy deny so vehemently Biff's assertion that *he* whistles in elevators? What do you think motivated Biff to say this about his father?

72. In the family discussion/argument that follows, describe Willy's attitude to Linda. Why does he treat her as he does here?

73. Based on what Biff said earlier when he was talking to Happy, do you believe that Bill Oliver "always" said he would "stake" Biff? Explain your answer.

74. How feasible is the marketing idea that Happy outlines? [Examine in particular his line, "We train a couple of weeks, and put on a couple of exhibitions, see?"] You might make notes on the pros and cons of the proposal in two columns.

75. Willy gives Biff two sets of entirely different (and totally inconsistent) advice about how to present himself to Bill Oliver. In two columns, make a list of the conflicting advice that Willy gives. Explain what you consider to be good and what you consider to be bad advice.

76. After Willy goes off to bed, Linda tells Biff, "It takes so little to make him happy." What does this tell us about the way in which Linda is trying to get her husband through his present problems?

77. In what ways does the idea that Biff will be able to get a substantial loan from Bill Oliver allow *both* Happy and Willy to retreat back into fantasies of the past when (it seems to them now) they were content with their lives?

78. What is the effect produced by having Biff visible in the cellar during Willy and Linda's closing dialogue?

Notes
"Filene's": "Filene's Basement, also called The Basement, was a Massachusetts-based chain of department stores" (Wikipedia article). It first opened in 1909 and survived into the first decade of the twenty-first century.
"the Hub": This is a 'nickname' for Boston. It is short for "The Hub of the Universe."
"Slattery's, Boston": E. T. Slattery was a high-end store in downtown *Boston* in the 19th and 20th selling men's, women's and children's clothing.
"that Ebbets Field game": "Ebbets Field was a Major League Baseball stadium in the Crown Heights, Brooklyn section of Brooklyn ... known mainly as the home of the Brooklyn Dodgers baseball team ... from 1913 to 1957, but was also home to three National Football League teams in the 1920s. Ebbets Field was demolished in 1960 and replaced by apartment buildings" (Wikipedia article). I could find no evidence that it ever staged high school football, even championship games.
"Hercules": Roman god famous for his strength and his many adventures including his Twelve Labors.

Commentary

Standing in the yard, Willy has heard most of the conversation in the house, and he is angry at the things Biff has said. However, it is worth noting that Biff has spoken about Willy only truths that Willy himself has earlier, in moments of honesty, admitted to Linda. Note these similarities:

"Biff: So what? I like to whistle sometimes." and "Willy: Well, I figure, what the hell, life is short, a couple of jokes."

"Biff: They've laughed at dad for years..." and "Willy: ... people don't seem to take to me ... They seem to laugh at me ... I'm fat. I'm very – foolish to look at ..."

Above all, of course, Willy has heard Biff ask "What woman?" when his mother was describing one of his car accidents, and this has both reminded him that Biff knows about his infidelity and reanimated his guilt for having cheated on Linda. (Interestingly, Biff never uses the word "crazy" to describe his father, though both Happy and Biff speak as though he had done so.) It is the truth of what he has heard that makes Willy so angry: he must deny it because to acknowledge its truth would be to accept the error of his dream and all that has flowed from it. To reject Biff's truths, Willy must deny the most fundamental part of his psyche: the maker of things; the carpenter; the person who actually enjoys the manual work he does. Absurdly, Willy claims that "Even your grandfather was better than a carpenter," and that he, "never in my life whistled in an elevator!" He is denying both his true heritage and his essential self.

Willy boasts about his contacts in the same way he did fifteen years earlier, "Go to Fileve's, go to the Hub, go to Slattery's, Boston. Call out the name

Willy Loman and see what happens! Big shot!" [Compare, "… they know me boys … The finest people … I have friends … I never have to wait in line to see a buyer, 'Willy Loman is here!' That's all they have to know, and I go right through."] It was not true then, and it certainly is not true now, but Biff (like Linda) conspires to perpetuate the illusion. Faced with a crisis, Biff backs down. Without hope in his own career, Willy must find hope in Biff or face the reality of his own failure. Harold Bloom defines Biff's dilemma in this way, "To save his father Biff must take on a filial task that threatens his own survival…" (*Guides* 42).

Up until this point, Willy's mind has escaped reality (not entirely successfully) in memories of a more prosperous and hopeful past, but the mention of Biff's plan to see Bill Oliver immediately gives him hope for a better future – a future in which Biff will finally achieve the success he predicted for him and their fractured relationship will be healed. As Linda will say later, "It takes so little to make him happy." Willy immediately begins to distort the situation, repeatedly (and very rudely) cutting Linda out of a business discussion because business is a man's world. Biff tries to be honest with his father, but Willy immediately interrupts him because the facts are not what he needs to hear. Willy needs to believe that Oliver has already agreed to back Biff, while Biff desperately tries to tell him he "didn't even see him yet…"

The discussion seems to have reached an impasse when Happy outlines his "feasible idea" for the Loman Brothers line of sporting goods. Each person sees in the proposal what he needs to see. To Willy, it is the sort of idea that spells almost instant business success, "Million-dollar … Lick the world!" To Happy and Biff, it is being in business without the constraints of being an employee. Happy tells Biff, "… it wouldn't be like a business. We'd be out playin' ball again … you wouldn't get fed up with it Biff…" Yet for all three, "It'd be the family again." The fantasy is of a return to the way things were fifteen years ago – a fantasy in which all three men can share. Biff (and by reflection Happy) can relive their days of athletic glory, and Willy can relive the days when he was (at least in his own mind) Frank Wagner's top salesman. It is, quite literally, a childish idea.

Willy immediately takes over the discussion, repeatedly cutting Linda off. Badaracco comments, "Linda tries several times to say something about the Loman Brothers line of sporting goods. Willy, fearing she will inject a dose of common sense, repeatedly and rudely cuts her off" (Lerner and Lerner ed. 97). Willy dictates how Biff should approach Oliver. His advice, however, shows the old contradictions that originate in his divided psyche: he tells Biff, "Walk in very serious … Be quiet, fine, serious. Everybody likes a kidder, but nobody lends him money," which is actually good advice, but seconds later he says, "Walk in with a big laugh … Start off with a couple of your good stories to lighten things up ... personality always wins the day." The earlier advice represents what Willy knows to be true of those (like Charley and Bernard) who *are* successful in business, and the latter represents his *belief* in the overriding importance of personality that he derived from his very partial knowledge of his father and brother.

Tensions rise over Willy's repeatedly rude and disrespectful treatment of Linda in the conversation. Willy degrades and insults her, and Biff is protective of his mother because he knows of Willy's ultimate act of betrayal with The Woman. However, under Linda's influence, Biff agrees to placate Willy. In private, even Happy acknowledges the truth about his father telling Biff, "let's face it: he's no hot-shot selling man," but he immediately retreats into sentimental fantasy when he adds, "Except that sometimes, you have to admit, he's a sweet personality." Absolutely *nothing* that the audience has seen in the play justifies Happy's assessment of Willy.

The subsequent action points again to the disconnect between reality and Willy's conflicted response to it. Linda complains that the shower is dripping, and Willy responds by venting about the low standard of the product, "Goddam plumbing, oughta be sued, those people. I hardly finished putting it in and the thing..." Nothing is ever Willy's fault. When Linda very reasonably questions whether Bill Oliver will remember Biff (she appears not to know about Biff's theft of the basketballs), Willy dismisses her concern. Continuing to place emphasis on appearance and personality over education and actual achievement, he says, "Wait'll Oliver gets a look at him." Now, he completely contradicts his earlier view of Biff's years of wandering saying, "Greatest thing in the world for him was to bum around." Willy does not give Biff advice about how to present his plan to start a sporting goods company but on how to *sell himself.* As before, he rudely cuts off Linda's contributions, but this time Biff restrains his urge to defend his mother. Feeling that Biff has once again taken on his role as favorite son and savior of the family, Happy desperately tries to get some attention by saying, "I'm gonna get married, Mom. I wanted to tell you." Linda, who has heard it all before, does not respond as Happy would have wished.

Left alone, Willy remembers Biff's finest moment, the championship game at Ebbets Field. He retains his faith that "A star like that, magnificent, can never really fade away." However, he deflects Linda's question, "[W]hat has he got against you[?]" and stares at the moon – a fitting symbol for the fragile hope he has put into Biff's meeting with Oliver. Linda's song becomes "*desperate but monotonous humming*" – symbolizing the tenuous nature of her hopes of saving Willy. What the audience *sees* is Biff disconnecting the tubing from the gas tap – a symbol of the fact that Willy's life or death literally rests in Biff's hands and on the outcome of his meeting with Bill Oliver – a meeting which the audience already knows can *never* live up to the expectations which the characters have piled upon it.

ACT TWO

Real Time Dialogue between Willy and Linda ("Willy: Wonderful coffee." to "Linda: Be careful!")

79. Describing how Biff looked that morning, Linda tells Willy, "He's so handsome in that suit. He could be a – anything in that suit!" What do you think that Linda was going to say and why did she cut herself off?
80. For once, because he is hopeful, Willy fantasizes about an idyllic future rather than an idyllic past. What are his dreams and how does the text make clear that they are totally unrealistic?
81. Willy's line, "Once in my life I would like to own something outright before its broken!" is not particularly original, but it is (unintentionally) very funny. Explain the element of paranoia in his description of purchasing appliances on the installment plan. How does this relate to the wider theme of how Willy relates to the modern business world?
82. What positive aspect of their financial situation does Linda point out? Comment on Willy's contradictory reaction to what she says.
83. How does Willy react when he learns that his sons "'want to blow him to a big meal'"?
84. Comment on the way that Linda checks that Willy has everything before he goes out. How is she treating him?

Notes

"General Electric": A huge firm making appliances for the home and for industry.
"a Hastings refrigerator": Not a real company.
"Frank's Chop House on Forty-eighth near Sixth Avenue": Miller may have in mind Frank's Famous Restaurant: Oyster and Chop House in New York.

Commentary

The music that is heard is not identified as the "*small and fine*" melody of the flute but as the "*gay and bright*" music of contemporary America. With Biff finally pursuing a career in business, Willy is confident that his vision of the capitalist entrepreneur as the new embodiment of the American Dream is about to be vindicated. Willy expresses his confidence that his son is "heading for a change," and Linda feeds his euphoric mood because she seems genuinely to share it. (We later learn that she is under the mistaken apprehension that Willy has taken away the rubber pipe from the cellar.)

Willy is optimistic about the future for the first time in the play, but as he always does, he quickly looses touch with reality. His desire to plant seeds (seeds which, Linda gently reminds him, will not germinate because "not enough sun gets back there. Nothing'll grow anymore") symbolizes his desire for continuity, his desperate need to create some tangible legacy to pass onto his sons. It also shows his unconscious desire to reconnect with nature. This self-contradictory motivation is developed when Willy outlines even more unrealistic dreams of buying "a little place out in the country" where he will "raise some vegetables, a couple of chickens." The life that he dreams of is the very antithesis of the life that he has led in Brooklyn – it is, in fact, much closer to the life that Biff has envisaged for himself on his own ranch.

When Willy talks of using his "many fine tools" to build "two guest houses" for Biff and Happy and their families, his is again unaware that he is conflating two contradictory impulses: his love of building things with his own hands and his desire to found a business dynasty. Thus, his hopeful plans illustrate both how ill-suited Willy is to the profession he chose, because it stifles his natural inclinations, and yet how he remains committed to that choice: he will only allow himself to retire to the country when he, and through him his sons, have *achieved* something in the city.

Willy's mood changes instantly when Linda brings him back to reality: the vital importance of getting Howard to agree to a New York job and the need for "a little advance" because they need "about two hundred dollars" to pay their outstanding bills. Inevitably, Willy sees this as evidence of his own failure as a provider, but he deflects the blame onto the appliances denouncing their shoddiness, "Once in my life I would like to own something outright before it's broken!" Interestingly, he is complaining about the very thing that, as a salesman, he relies upon – repeat purchases. He simply does not see the connection between his own situation and that of the customers who buy the product that he sells. In fact, he speaks like the craftsman he fundamentally is – a man who builds well and builds to last.

Ironically, the Lomans' financial situation is not quite as bad as it seems to be for, as Linda points out, they are about to make "the last payment on the mortgage." Willy shares his wife's pride in their achievement, but he is even prouder of, "All the cement, the lumber, the reconstruction I put in this house!" Once again, however, this is not enough. In contrast with Linda, who believes that the purpose of the house was to provide a place to raise their family, Willy needs Biff to "take this house, and raise a family." This is not the pioneering dream; it is actually a reaction against the life Willy led as a child (traveling in a wagon and ultimately being abandoned by his father). This is the dream of middle class America in the mid-twentieth century – the dream of amounting to something.

Willy is immediately cheered when Linda tells him about the boys' plans for a celebration dinner. That symbolizes for him the family he has always wanted to build, and he has a surge of confidence that he can "knock Howard for a loop." The sight of Linda's mended stockings, however, brings to mind Will's guilt over his adultery. It is a reminder of just how dishonest and fragile Willy's plans are.

Real Time Telephone Call between Linda and Biff ("Linda: Hello? Oh Biff! ... Good-bye, Biff dear.")

85. What might be symbolized by the fact that Linda discovers it was Biff not Willy who removed the rubber pipe?
86. What is Biff actually doing at the time he calls home? What does this foreshadow about his meeting with Bill Oliver?

Commentary

The function of this little scene is to confront illusions with a solid dose of reality. Even when Biff destroys Linda's hope that Willy took away the rubber tubing by telling her that it was he who removed it, she remains hopeful telling Biff, "I'm not worried darling, because this morning he left in such high spirits, it was like the old days! I'm not afraid anymore." Linda is living in denial; she has been caught up in the unfounded optimism of her husband and her sons, but she (of all people) *ought* to know better. The time must be at least ten thirty, and Biff is still waiting to see Oliver, who obviously does not remember his name. Nevertheless, Linda tells him, that Willy "may have big news too!" which is proof that she still believes both that Oliver will lend Biff $10,000 and that Howard will give Willy a New York job. Linda's love for Willy is clear from her description of him as "a little boat looking for a harbor," and she remains confident that Biff will "save his life." The audience knows that both Biff and Willy (and therefore also Linda) are heading for devastating failure.

Real Time Dialogue between Willy and Howard ("Willy: Pst! Pst!" to "Howard: There's people outside.")

87. Contrast the manner in which Willy approaches Howard with the advice (admittedly contradictory advice) that he gave Biff on how he should approach Bill Oliver.
88. How does the way that Howard talks about buying and using the wire recorder emphasize the radically different lifestyles of employer and employee?
89. What can you infer about the promise that Howard made to Willy at the Christmas party?
90. Willy agrees with Howard's statement that "business is business," but the two men have a radically different understanding of what the phrase means. What does it mean to Howard?
91. Willy describes the moment in his life when he decided not to go to Alaska during the gold rush but to seek his future in selling (though whether he ever seriously considered going to Alaska may be doubted). In Willy's account he had an epiphany, and it was prompted by knowing about Dave Singleman. What aspects of Singleman's life and career convinced Willy to stick with selling? In reaching this decision, what aspects of Singleman's life and death does Willy seem to have ignored.

92. As well as reminding Howard of his promise at the Christmas party, w other reasons does Willy give why his boss *should* find him a "spot" in New York? How does Howard react to what Willy says about his past relationship with Howard's father and his past service to the company?
93. What is the significance of Willy's reaction when he accidentally turns on the wire recorder?
94. Why does Howard fire Willy? What does his doing so reveal about his inability to empathize with Willy's situation and feelings?
95. Explain why Willy cannot bring himself to "throw" himself on his sons.

Notes

"wire-recording machine": Reel to reel wire recorders using thin magnetic steel wire were invented in 1898. They were used for office dictation purposes and also home entertainment, since the reproductive quality was high. They were superseded in the early 1950s by tape recorders.

Commentary

Howard and Willy inhabit two very different worlds. Howard represents progress and innovation, contemporary business practice and the wealthy employer-class, while Willy struggles to keep up with technology, admires what he believes to be traditional business values, and is a struggling employee. The wire-recorder symbolizes technological innovation and novelty. It excites Howard who has already mastered its use and seen its potential applications in business and leisure; he is more interested in his machine than he is in his human employee Willy. In contrast, when later in the scene Willy "*accidentally switches on the recorder,*" he panics "*leaping away in fright*" and shouts for Howard to "Shut it off!" Like his inability to control his car, there could hardly be a better illustration of Willy's fear that the future will run out of his control; the business world is changing, and he is too old and inflexible to change with it.

The wire-recorder also points to other differences between Howard and Willy. The voice recordings of his wife, son and daughter reveal a tight-knit, loving family, of which Howard is very evidently the commanding figure – the kind of family that Willy can only dream of having once had. The machine also reveals the economic gulf between the Wagner and Loman families. When Howard says, "they're only a hundred and a half," he seems completely oblivious to the fact that this is way out of Willy's financial reach. He then explains, "So you tell the maid to turn the radio on when Jack Benny comes on…," as though Willy too can afford a maid. Financially secure himself, Howard is incapable of understanding how economically vulnerable Willy is. In fact, one of the reasons Howard does not feel too bad about firing Willy is that he believes Biff and Happy are far more successful than they actually are because this is the impression Willy has always given him. He advises, "This is no time for pride, Willy. You go to your sons and you tell them you're tired. You've got two great boys, haven't you?" and Willy is trapped by his own deceptions because, even at this moment, he cannot bring himself to be honest but must continue to act as though his sons are both "working on a very big deal."

Willy's approach to his interview with Howard follows none of his advice (either good or bad) to Biff: he is neither serious and dignified, nor does he come in with a laugh and a good story. He is, from the start, apologetic, self-effacing and obsequious, allowing Howard entirely to dominate the conversation. The wealthy Howard does not respect Willy, repeatedly cutting him off (just as Willy does to Linda) and patronizingly calling him "kid" despite the fact that Willy is almost twice his age. (This word use is much more significant than Howard realizes, for Willy has truly never grown up; he is still, despite the evidence of a lifetime of failure, the impressionable, idealistic adolescent who encountered Dave Singleman. Charley asks him, "Willy, when are you going to grow up?") When Howard's lighter falls on the floor, Willy automatically picks it up and hands it to him, the very reverse of the advice he gave Biff, "And if anything falls off the desk while you're talking to him – like a parcel or something – don't you pick it up. They have office boys for that." Willy is exposed as a phony temperamentally incapable of impressing anyone with the force of his personality.

Howard evidently has no recollection of having promised to try to "think of some spot for" Willy in New York (just as Bill Oliver will have no recollection of Biff) suggesting that Willy gave their conversation (*if* it ever happened) much more significance than it actually had. The man who advised his son, "Don't be so modest. You always started too low ... don't undersell yourself. No less than fifteen thousand dollars," pleads with Howard that "If I could take home – well, sixty-five dollars a week, I could swing it." As the conversation progresses, he comes down, "all I need to set my table is fifty dollars a week," and down, "If I had forty dollars a week – that's all I'd need." The problem is that Willy is selling himself (i.e., his labor), and neither the product nor the salesman is much good.

Howard has evidently never even considered giving Willy a job in New York. There is a personal element to this decision: throughout their dialogue, it is clear that Howard finds Willy irritating. Finance is also involved: to make Willy a floor salesman in New York would mean putting him back on a salary, and it is clear to Howard that Willy is not productive enough to justify this. Howard flatters Willy by projecting back to him Willy's own version of himself: he is "a road man" and Wagner's does "a road business"; there is no question that Willy "can sell merchandise," but "everybody's got to pull his own weight." Everybody can lie to Willy because Willy lies to and about himself.

By keeping Willy on commission, the firm only pays him a percentage of his gross sales. This has seemed like a reasonable compromise to Howard, who is not a completely uncaring man nor one without some loyalty to a long-serving employee, but Willy's failure to keep his appointment with Brown and Morrison (just the latest such failure) means that he is damaging the firm's reputation and that could cost the Wagner Company revenue. The fact is, as he finally admits to Willy, "I don't want you to represent us. I've been meaning to tell you for a long time now." Willy's erratic behavior in their interview finally prompts (or provides an excuse for) Howard to act.

Willy tries to appeal to Howard's emotional side – he has, after all, served the firm for thirty-four years. He reminds Howard that when he was born his father asked Willy what he "thought of the name Howard." (In his later conversation with Charley this will metamorphose into the claim that he named Howard, which is simply not true.) The two men agree that "Business is definitely business," but they mean something entirely different by the phrase. For Howard, it means the bottom line: business is a profit/loss account and decisions are based on data – although Howard is not in reality so unfeeling as his own words would suggest. For Willy, business is based on being liked, on loyalty and on personal connections, intangible factors that do not appear on the firm's balance sheet.

The apotheosis of everything in which Willy believes is expressed in the myth of the drummer Dave Singleman, a man whose personality inspired "respect, and comradeship, and gratitude." Old Dave was well liked both by his fellow drummers and his buyers, to whom he could sell simply by picking up the phone in his hotel room, and when he died, "hundreds of salesmen and buyers were at his funeral." That is what Willy wanted for himself when he decided to make a career in sales, to "be remembered and loved and helped by so many different people." However, even putting aside the inconsistencies and improbabilities of the story of Singleman (a man alone with no family who was still working at age eighty-four and left no tangible legacy to anyone), Willy has to admit to Howard that, in so far as he ever approached Singleman's status, the people he knew have retired or died and the men who have replaced them, "don't know me anymore."

Far from winning Howard over, Willy's story actually prompts a firm rejection of his request and an attempt to brush him off because Howard has "got to see some people." Increasingly desperate, Willy retreats into a myth of his own past, specifically 1928 when he "averaged a hundred and seventy dollars a week in commissions" and when Frank Wagner put his hand on Willy's shoulder and "promises [were] made across this desk!" That this is total fantasy (the same sort of fantasy that has led Biff to believe that Bill Oliver "put his arm on my shoulder, and he said, 'Biff, if you ever need anything, come to me'") is evident from Howard's statement, "Now, Willy, you never averaged –," and from Willy's confusion about whether Frank came to him or he went to Frank's office. The anger that these memories have generated only confirms Howard's decision that Willy is a liability to the firm and must be fired. Willy has lost everything; he has lost his identity.

Willy's Third Imaginative Recreation of the Past ("Willy: Oh, Ben, how did you do it?" to "Willy: Right between the goal posts.")

96. In his own mind, Willy remembers the second time that he had a chance to go to Alaska. What two (conflicting) attractions does Ben's offer of a job there have for Willy?

97. Why is Linda against Willy giving up his job and relocating the family to Alaska? Consider the possibility that in his memory Willy is merely projecting his own reasons onto his wife.

98. Why does Willy finally reject Ben's offer telling him, "We'll do it here … We're gonna do it here!"?

99. Explain why Willy considers the Ebbets Field game to be so vitally important to Biff's future.

100. It is clear that Charley is kidding Willy about the Ebbets Field game. Why is he doing that?

101. Comment on Willy's line, "Eighty thousand people!"

Notes

"Red Grange": Harold Edward 'Red' Grange (1903-1991), "nicknamed 'The Galloping Ghost', was an American football halfback for the University of Illinois, the Chicago Bears, and for the short-lived New York Yankees" (Wikipedia article). Significantly, after his retirement, Grange (forty-six at the time the play was first produced in 1949) made money in the insurance business.

"Eighty thousand people!": C.1930, Ebbets Field had a capacity of 32,000, although later this expanded to a maximum of 35,000 (Wikipedia article). Willy's memory typically distorts the past.

Commentary

Once Willy sought relief from an unendurable present by conjuring up an idealized version of the past, but now he can no longer separate past from present. Willy wants Ben to tell him the secret of success, but (as always) he gets no answer to his present-day question. Instead, the scene supposedly represents Willy's memory of a very brief visit that Ben made to Brooklyn following his business trip to Alaska when Ben offered his brother the chance to move to Alaska, a wild, lawless region where Willy and his sons could "screw up … [their] fists and … fight for a fortune." His memory allows Willy to present himself as enthusiastic about the proposition and to shift the blame for his failure to take up Ben's offer onto Linda, who tells Ben her husband has "got a beautiful job here," and Willy that he's "doing well enough."

In this scene Willy's mind projects onto Linda the side of Willy's personality that rejects the idea of great wealth achieved through adventurous risk-taking in favor of a more apparently secure, certainly more modest, success in selling. In his memory, it is Linda who convinces Willy that he is "building something with this firm," using Frank Wagner's promise as evidence. When Ben rightly points out that Willy is building nothing tangible, nothing he can hold (like gold and diamonds) in his hand, Linda reminds him of the intangible values of Dave Singleman. In Willy's memory, Linda is responsible for limiting his ambition and specifically for him not taking up Ben's offer – something which he comes to regret. What actually happened during Ben's visit (assuming that it even happened) it is impossible to know.

In his memory, Willy is finally convinced that he is doing the right thing. He tells Ben, "We'll do it here ... We're gonna do it here!" Aware that he himself is never going to be rich, Willy takes refuge in the illusion that he is grooming Biff to take his place at "the lunch table at the Commodore Hotel" where businessmen discuss the whole "wealth of Alaska." What Willy ignores is the fact that the people around that table are the sons of people like Ben who have been born into wealth. He is deluded in believing that Biff will also end up "with diamonds ... on the basis of being liked ... [because] when he walks into a business office his name will sound like a bell and all the doors will open to him!" When Willy turns to Ben for confirmation that he has found the key to success, however, Ben does not give it. Instead he insists, "There's a new continent at your doorstep William. You could walk out rich," and then vanishes.

Willy insists defiantly that he will make his and his family's fortune in the city, and takes refuge in a memory of the high point of his past optimism, the preparations for the Ebbets Field game. Biff emerges as a superior being; Happy and Bernard vie for the honor of carrying his helmet. Willy is convinced that his son "comin' home ... captain of the All-Scholastic Championship Team" will be the key to his future success in business, and Biff also believes this. He hero-worships Willy, reminding him that "when I take off my helmet, that touchdown is for you."

Charley uses humor to bring Willy's expectations down to earth by pretending to know nothing about the game in which Biff will be playing. Willy cannot deal with Charley mocking the importance he has placed on creating an impression through football and gets very angry offering to fight Charley. Remembering that Willy's imaginative reconstructions of the past are always informed by his knowledge of the present, Willy's impotent anger (impotent because Charley has no intention of fighting with him) signifies his subconscious knowledge that Charley is right. Willy ends in complete fantasy remembering Biff's touchdown "Right between the goalposts" in front of

"Eighty thousand people!" The idyll of that Saturday afternoon fades (just as its promise soon faded), and Willy finds himself railing in the corridor outside of Charley's office.

Real Time Dialogue between Willy, Bernard and Charley ("Jenny: Say Bernard..." to "Charley: Jesus!")

102. What inferences can you draw from Jenny's statement, "I can't deal with him any more, and your father gets upset every time he comes."

103. Willy is said to be *"surprised"* and *"almost shocked"* when he first sees Bernard. Explain why.

104. Contrast the way in which Bernard talks about himself to the way Willy talks about Biff.

105. Willy tells Bernard that the question of why Biff did not go to summer school to make up his grade "has been trailing me like a ghost for the last fifteen years." A moment later he adds, "It keeps going round in my mind, maybe I did something to him." Is Willy being sincere when he says this? To put it another way: Is Willy deceiving Bernard or himself?

106. Explain exactly why Biff had "given up [on] his life" after Boston and why Willy reacts as he does to Bernard's question, "What happened in Boston, Willy?"

107. Explain why it is impossible for Willy to take Bernard's advice "sometimes, Willy, it's better for a man to just walk away" (which sounds very similar to Charley's earlier advice, "When a deposit bottle is broken you don't get your nickel back").

108. Is it true that Charley "never told him [Bernard] what to do ... never took any interest in him"? Are those two things the same (as Willy appears to think they are)?

109. Comment on the accuracy of Willy's claim to have "named" Howard. (Go back in the text to what Willy told Howard.)

110. Exactly how is Charley's view of the business world different from that of Willy? What precisely does Charley mean when he says, "The only thing you got in this world is what you can sell"? In what way is Willy's view of business disastrously idealistic?

111. Compare and contrast Charley's view of business with that of Howard Wagner.

112. Although he may not be fully conscious of it yet, Willy has a tragic, life-changing epiphany. He tells Charley, "you end up worth more dead than alive." Charley replies, "Willy, nobody's worth nothin' dead." Explain the different meaning that each man is giving to the word "worth." What does Willy's statement foreshadow?

Notes

"J. P. Morgan": John Pierpont Morgan Sr. (1837-1913) was the son of a successful American financier and banker who became the dominant figure in American capitalism from the 1870s until his death.

Commentary

Jenny, Charley's secretary, makes it clear that Willy is a frequent and a disruptive visitor. Presumably he comes to Charley's office every week to borrow $50 so that he can keep it secret from Linda. Jenny says, "I can't deal with him anymore," implying that Willy's emotional instability is getting progressively worse. She also tells Bernard, "you father gets all upset everytime he comes," which emphasizes the emotional toll that trying to keep Willy from self-destructing is taking on Charley (just as it is on Linda).

The audience shares Willy's shock at the adult Bernard since he bears no relation to the Bernard of Willy's 'memories' – the only Bernard we have seen on stage to this point. He is, in fact, everything that Willy anticipated that Biff would be: rich and successful, mixing with "fine people," a family man with two children, and (most amazing of all) a sportsman. Bernard is also the antithesis of everything Willy taught Biff, for he is understated, reserved and modest about his achievements. He tells Willy only that the reason he is going to Washington is "just a case I've got there," and it is only later that Charley tells Willy that that case is before the Supreme Court of the United States. Intimidated by Bernard's obvious success, Willy lies about Biff's success in the West and his reasons for coming back East. However, there is now something mechanical in Willy lies. He uses the word "big" three times, and the statement that Bill Oliver called Biff in from the West, "Long distance, carte blanche, special deliveries" gets progressively less and less meaningful. (Is Biff a parcel?) As has happened before, the lies and self-deception implode, collapsing on their own feeble structure, and Willy asks Bernard the same question he has asked Ben, "What – what's the secret?"

That question can be answered on two levels. Bernard suggests that Biff never made it because, "He never trained himself for anything." Willy vehemently denies this stating that "After high school he took so many correspondence courses. Radio mechanics, television: God knows what, and never made the slightest mark." Both Bernard and Willy are to some extent correct. Not getting a university education was *a* determining factor in Biff's failure (correspondence courses are simply no substitute), but it was not *the* determining factor: Biff could still have made something of himself. Biff failed math because Willy had instilled the belief that football and being popular were more important than getting good grades in school, but failing to graduate was something that Biff could have easily remedied.

The determining factor was that, after his visit to Boston to see his father, Biff no longer *believed in his ability* to succeed in the business world because he had seen that his father's success was a lie. Bernard pinpoints the specific moment when Biff's attitude toward his own future success changed, but he cannot account for that change. Willy keeps pushing Bernard for an answer, but when Bernard asks, "What happened in Boston, Willy?" he is immediately defensive. He challenges Bernard, "What are you trying to do, blame it on me? If a boy lays down is that my fault?" Willy must place the blame for Biff's failure on his son's faulty character, because the alternative is to accept that his own dream was an error and that he was responsible for setting Biff up to fail.

It is not easy to understand the psychology of Willy's denial of the events in Boston. He seems genuinely to have forgotten what happened. That is the only way to explain a line of questioning that leads directly to Boston and to his personal responsibility. Freud would explain it as a repressed memory, buried in the subconscious, literally tearing the psyche apart, but not available to the consciousness. In terms of classical tragedy, it is like Oedipus's discovery of something that he knew all along, that a mortal could not oppose the will of the gods, that, despite all that he did to ensure that Apollo's prophesy that he would kill his father and marry his mother, "It has all come true," and that he must take moral responsibility for his actions. In this scene, Willy comes perhaps closer than anywhere in the play to realizing his own responsibility for Biff's failure, "It keeps going around in my mind, maybe I did something to him. I got nothing to give him," but unlike Oedipus (or Macbeth or Othello), he retreats into self-deception because the truth would destroy him.

Two things shock Willy about Bernard: that he never mentioned arguing a case before SCOTUS, and that his father "never told him what to do ... never took any interest in him." Charley provides an answer to the first puzzle that points to the reason for Willy's constant boasting about his own success and that of his boys, "He don't have to [talk about it] – he's gonna do it." Charley does not, however, intend to hurt Willy's feelings by this statement. We can see this when he accepts Willy's second point, "My salvation is that I never took any interest in anything." This is self-evidently not true. Charley instilled in Bernard clear moral values and an ethic of hard work. What he *did not do* was to try to remake Bernard in his own image. In addition, Charley is showing his care for Willy even at this moment. In an effort to keep the interview (an interview that will upset him) short, he mentions that he has "got an accountant inside," but Willy needs to talk. He also needs more than $50.

Charley's success is tangible proof of the error of Willy's philosophy of business. Charley is a realist who adheres to the same business principles as Howard Wagner: success is defined not by intangible factors but by sales accounts. In their conversation, Charley confronts Willy with uncomfortable truths: Willy could make $50 a week working in New York for Charley (not a great wage, but sufficient for his needs), but his jealous pride prevents him from doing so; the values Willy has believed in (loyalty, being liked, etc.) "don't mean anything" in business; and the people who succeed in business are not people who are liked. Charley points to the irony that Willy is "a salesman" who does not know that "The only thing you got in this world is what you can sell," and Willy has nothing to sell anymore.

Willy rejects a secure job rather than acknowledge that everything he has believed about the American business world is false. Once again, Willy steps back from the epiphany of the traditional tragic hero, the moment of self-understanding and self-condemnation, taking refuge in the illusion that he is merely borrowing money from Charley that he will repay.

Willy admits that Charley is "the only friend I got. Isn't that a remarkable thing?" In this moment, Willy sees the failure of his own dreams, but he does so *without* seeing the phony nature of the dream itself. It suddenly strikes Willy that, "After all the highways, and the trains, and the appointments, and the years, you end up worth more dead than alive." Here, Willy is compounding his tragic error: he still defines "worth" in terms of success, influence and wealth, so he measures the value of his own life purely in financial terms. In his reply, Charley defines "worth" in terms of those intangible factors in which Willy has always believed: loyalty, friendship, and obligation. He says, "Willy, nobody's worth nothin' dead … Did you hear what I said?" Willy hears, but he does not listen.

Why does Charley act as he does, repeatedly offering Willy a job and repeatedly being insulted by Willy's refusal to work for him? Charley himself tells Willy, "I know you don't like me, and nobody can say I'm in love with you, but I'll give you a job because – just for the hell of it, put it that way." Many critics take Charley at his word, but here he is trying to make the job offer more acceptable to Willy by making it appear *not to be* an act of charity and sympathy, so that Willy can accept without having his feelings hurt. The truth is that Charley both likes and loves Willy, and that Willy likes and loves Charlie, though his jealousy prevents him from acknowledging his feelings. As the SparkNotes editors perceptively conclude, "Ironically, Charley is the only person to offer Willy a business opportunity on the strength of a personal bond."

Real Time at Frank's Chop House ("Stanley: That's all right…" to "Biff: I can't talk to him!")

113. What attitude to women is implicit in Happy's statement, "Strudel's comin'"? (Strudel is a baked confection of thin, layered pastry with a sweet fruit filling – most commonly apple.)
114. What might Happy be wanting to know when he asks the girl, "You don't happen to sell, do you?"?
115. What can we infer from the girl's claim to have been on "a lot of" magazine covers?
116. What lies does Happy tell Miss Forsythe in order to impress her?

117. What, in Happy's mind, is "a shame" about the beautiful Miss Forsythe? How is this linked (in his mind) to the fact that he "can't [bring himself] to get married"?

118. Biff describes the life-changing epiphany that he had when Bill Oliver finally appeared and, "Didn't remember who I was or anything," and later when he realizes that he had stolen Oliver's pen. What truth about himself does this lead Biff to finally confront?

119. Explain Biff's determination to make his father acknowledge the truth. What does Biff's statement, "He thinks I've been spiting him all these years and it's eating him up" tell you about what motivates his desire to save Willy.

120. Happy also wants to save his father, but his method is very different. How does he react to Biff's determination to tell Willy "what a ridiculous lie my whole life has been!"?

121. How do both Willy and Happy manipulate Biff away from telling him "cold facts ... – instances – facts ... facts about my life" to telling him something hopeful – something that Willy can believe, even though he knows, as much as do Biff and Happy, that it is not true?

122. At the end of the scene, Biff cries, "Listen, will you let me out of it, will you just let me out of it!" To what do you think that the pronoun "it" refers?

Notes

"Hackensack": Hackensack is a city in New Jersey. In this phrase, Hackensack stands for a small, backward, poor kind of hick town.

"hit a number or somethin'?": The numbers game, or racket, is an lottery played mostly in poor and working class neighborhoods. With the legalization of state lotteries (beginning in 1964), it has virtually disappeared.

"Strudel": A confection of layered puff pastry with a sweet filling (normally fruit).

"West Point": The United States Military Academy (USMA) – an elite military training school.

Commentary

Up to this point, the emphasis of the play has been on Biff's character flaws and business failures. At the start of this scene the focus is, briefly, on Happy. Ironically, Happy has completely and uncritically internalized Willy's values and strategies, while Biff has (in a limited and incomplete way) rejected them. Unlike Willy, Happy *does* seem to have the knack of being liked, though he has discovered by hard experience that making a personal impression is no guarantee of advancement in the firm for which he works. Aware of his lowly position (as Willy is aware of his low sales), he lies about his success as Willy does, though with much more panache and plausibly. He tells Stanley that his brother is a "big cattle man" who "I think ... pulled off a big deal today"; he tells Miss Forsythe that he is a champagne salesman who went to West Point and that his brother is the quarterback with the New York Giants.

Denied power in the business world, Happy compensates by using his good looks and sexual magnetism as a means of gaining control over women. Although he knows nothing of his father's infidelity, he (like Willy) seduces women to convince himself of his own agency. Happy has no respect for women, a characteristic he has picked up from Willy's continual disrespect for Linda. Women are "Strudel"; he immediately objectifies Miss Forsythe, telling Stanley, "Look at that mouth. Oh, God. And the binoculars." In her analysis of this scene Kay Stanton argues that in picking up two attractive young women, "Happy wishes to establish a safety net of sexual confidence to protect them [himself and Biff] against news of failure that he may anticipate and fear, and he perhaps wants unconsciously to show off his 'success' to contrast Biff's probably failure. Magnanimous Happy will give this choice female morsel to Biff if he only says he wants her – assuming in advance that she has no choice but to acquiesce" (Bloom ed. 134). When Biff arrives, he asks him, "Do you want her? She's on call," words that treat Miss Forsythe as a commodity. Happy enjoys demonstrating his power over women, as when he tells Miss Forsythe to call off her date, see if she can get a friend, and "Come back soon." When she leaves, Happy gloats over his success. He has reduced Miss Forsythe to a call girl, and he blames her for it: to him, she is really just a slut (of course, he does not use that word); in fact, all women are sluts, "There's not a good woman in a thousand." Hypocritically, Happy then takes the moral high ground explaining that the reason he can never marry is because he could never trust his wife to be faithful.

When Biff enters, it is immediately evident to the audience that something profound has happened to him. He tells Happy, "I want to tell Dad a couple of things and I want you to help me." It soon emerges that Biff wants to use truth to break the destructive cycle into which they have all been drawn. Today, he tells Happy, he learned that Bill Oliver did not remember him because he was never a salesman for Oliver, he was merely a shipping clerk. The decisive moment came when Biff found himself in Oliver's office stealing his pen. Biff says he "can't explain" his action, but the audience can: Biff has *always* stolen things (just as Happy has always 'stolen' women) because he cannot get these things legitimately. As he runs down the stairs, Biff finally gets it: he steals because he has been brought up to regard himself as *entitled* to succeed (just as Happy seduces his colleagues girlfriend's to compensate for the fact that they are, unjustly in Happy's opinion, higher up the corporate ladder than he is).

Biff now realizes that Willy's dream of success is self-destructive for the simple reason that neither Willy, Happy, nor himself are success material. None of them has what it takes to make it to the top (or to anywhere near the top) in business, and Biff wants to share this epiphany with his father. Biff now knows that he is not in any way remarkable; he realizes that they have all "been talking in a dream for fifteen years." He wants to break that dream by ceasing to present himself to the world as something he is not. He tells Happy, "I'm not the man somebody lends that kind of money to." Happy, like Linda, wants to give Willy hope, even though it is hope without any foundation in reality; he urges Biff to "tell him [Willy] something nice." He pressures Biff to give a positive account of his meeting with Bill Oliver because, "Dad is never so happy as when he's looking forward to something" – words that Linda could have spoken.

There is another vital element of Biff's motivation. He tells Happy that he must make Willy see the truth because, "He thinks I've been spiting him all these years and it's eating him up." Biff has realized that he has not failed in business as an act of personal revenge against his father. He has failed as an unconscious rebellion against a corrupting dream; he has failed because he never had the qualities needed to succeed in business; and he has failed because his natural inclination is to work with his hands in the great outdoors. Despite what happened in Boston, Biff has realized that he loves his father. He genuinely believes that understanding all this will liberate both of them: it will free Willy from the "ghost" of guilt over his adultery that has dogged him ever since, and from the sense of professional failure that is destroying him; and it will free Biff from trying to live a kind of life that can never satisfy him. In contrast, Happy (who has not realized that the dream is "phony") wants to keep Willy happy by perpetuating the illusion as long as possible.

Temporarily, Biff acquiesces, but he soon insists on sharing his epiphany with his father. He intends to present Willy with "cold fact … instances – facts … facts about my life" in the place of the lies they have told for years. Willy, however, uses emotional blackmail telling his sons that he was fired and dishonestly pretending that it is Linda who needs to hear "a little good news … because the woman has waited and the woman has suffered." He then virtually forces Biff to construct a hopeful narrative of his meeting with Oliver, "So don't give me a lecture about facts and aspects. I am not interested. Now what've you got to say to me?" Out of stories himself, Willy demands that Biff comes up with a story, and Biff knows he is trapped by his love for his father. Willy feeds him lines that Biff has to complete and then expands upon the positive narrative himself. Helpless, Biff shouts, "Dad, you're not letting me tell you what I want to tell you!" When he desperately begs, "Listen, will you let me out of it, will you just let me out of it!" the word "it" refers to Willy's dream of making it big in business on the force of one's personality. Biff wants out!

Frank's Chop House – in Willy's Mind Past and Present become Indistinguishable ("Young Bernard: Mrs. Loman" to "Stanley: ... Mr. Loman! Mr. Loman!")

123. Why does the imaginative recreation of the moment when Bernard told Linda that Biff had failed math and had left for Boston (a scene which cannot be a memory since Willy was not there to witness it) intrude into Willy's consciousness precisely when and how it does?

124. Biff knows that he is going to have to tell his father that Oliver is not going to back the Loman Brothers idea. Explain the compromise story that Biff comes up with – a story that he hopes will convince Willy that he still has the personality to impress a man like Oliver (and so potentially *other* businessmen) but will allow Biff to explain why he is not going to get the loan from Oliver?

125. The next imaginative recreation (one actually based on memory) to intrude into Willy's consciousness is about the moments immediately *before* Biff discovers him with The Woman. Why does this intrude into Willy's consciousness precisely when it does?

126. How does Miller contrive to get Willy offstage? Why is it essential to get him offstage?

127. Explain how Biff's attitude to Willy changes radically after he exits. What has caused the change?

128. Biff, perhaps trying to deal with his own feelings of guilt, turns on Happy who, in response, has two uncompleted lines, "What're you talking about, I'm the one who –" and "Me? Who goes away? Who runs off and –." It is pretty clear that in relation to looking after and showing concern for Willy, Happy is trying to establish his own innocence by pushing the blame onto Biff. How do you think Happy would have completed these two sentences?

129. Explain Happy's action in denying to the two young women that Willy is his father and telling them "we're going to paint this town!"

Notes

"Grand Central": Grand Central Station was at the height of its popularity at this time.

"Standish Arms": The Standish Arms Hotel is actually in Brooklyn Heights, New York, not Boston.

Commentary

Earlier in the play, Willy was able to separate the past and present, but he has been finding it progressively harder and harder to distinguish between them and now they co-exist in his mind as equal realities. As Biff tries to explain the harsh truth that he is "washed up with Oliver" because he never had the relationship with Oliver that Loman mythology claimed he had, Willy desperately tries to regain control of his present by interpreting the past. He is still trying to understand what it was that caused Biff to "lay down" after high school and how that explains his son's failure today, but this is impossible since he refuses to take any responsibility for Biff's failure. Instead of accepting that the turning point was Biff's visit to the hotel in Boston, he focuses on his son failing math as the source of his later failures. He turns on Biff saying, "*furiously*: If you hadn't flunked [math] you'd've been set by now!"

Learning that Biff stole Oliver's pen temporarily brings Willy out of the past – here, at last, is a fact that he cannot avoid. Both Biff and Happy, drawing on Willy's own teaching, try to justify Biff's action. Biff says, "I didn't exactly steal it!" and Happy adds, "He had it in his hand and just then Oliver walked in, so he got nervous and stuck it in his pocket." Based on Biff's earlier account of what happened, the audience knows that both statements are simply untrue. We know that Willy must take some responsibility for Biff's actions because when his son was a teen he consistently praised his initiative when he took things (e.g., when he took the football and pilfered building materials) and protected him from the consequences. Willy taught Biff that he did not have to follow the rules that lesser mortals follow, and Biff's subsequent behavior (e.g. stealing basketballs from Oliver and the theft that got him in jail) is a result of his parental conditioning. This is the truth that Willy must deny, for to accept it would destroy him.

The reality of the stolen pen, however, cannot be avoided, and this is why Willy's mind takes him back to the moment in the Boston hotel when he let Biff down in a way that destroyed the young boy's confidence in everything for which Willy had previously stood. Finally, Biff realizes that his father is reliving what happened. He is "*horrified*," and in a desperate attempt to protect Willy from the reemergence of that memory, he "*desperately*" lies to Willy. Briefly, it works, but, unlike Happy, who wants to elaborate the lie by confirming that Biff will have lunch with Oliver next day, Biff is determined to put an end to it. Maintaining the myth that Oliver has asked him to a meeting, Biff nevertheless tells Willy, "I'll make good somewhere, but I can't go tomorrow, see? ... I took those balls years ago, now I walk in with his pen? ... I can't face him like that!" Notice how Biff is careful to take personal responsibility for his failure, leaving Willy's values and aspirations (which he knows to be "phony") intact. However, Willy is unable to accept this compromise. He insists on blaming Biff's personal animus for his failure which goads Biff into stating the truth he has tried so hard to obfuscate, "I can't go. I've got no appointment." Ignoring his son's earlier efforts to meet him halfway in his fantasies, Willy insists that Biff is motivated by spite. The final barrier of repression has fallen, and Willy can no longer prevent himself from reliving the moment when he destroyed Biff's life.

Aware that he has probably shattered what remains of Willy's sanity, Biff guiltily pays tribute to him as "a prince ... a fine troubled prince. A hard-working prince." Angrily he turns on Happy saying, "I sense it, you don't give a good goddam about him." Defeated, Biff desperately pleads with Happy to "help him ... Help me, help me, I can't bear to look at his face!" Happy's reaction, however, confirms all that Biff has just said about him. By denying that Willy is his father, Happy shows that he will reject any truth that contradicts the narrative about himself that he has constructed. Seducing Miss Forsythe will confirm Happy's sense of his own agency, and it will temporarily obscure the reality of his many failures both as a man of business and as a son. Given that Happy has always taken second place in Willy's affections, his attitude, however, reprehensible, is understandable.

Willy's Fourth Imaginative Recreation of the Past ("Willy: Will you stop laughing" to "Willy: I'll whip you!")

130. What does The Woman mean when she tells Willy, "You ruined me"? [Note that he replies, "That's nice of you to say that."]
131. Willy's obstinate reluctance to answer the door can hardly be an accurate memory of what happened when he heard knocking on the door. Why not? So why *is* obstinate reluctance to answer the door a feature of his imaginative recreation?
132. What was Biff's intention in going to see his father in Boston? What does his action show about the way in which he regarded his father at that time?
133. Other than her simply being in his father's room (which would probably have been enough in itself), what aspects of the way that Willy handles the appearance of "Miss Francis" from his bathroom add to Biff's disillusion with his father?
134. Explain why, following this incident, Biff did not go to summer school and retake math, did not succeed in any of the correspondence courses he took, stole his way out of every job he ever had, and finally left home.

Commentary

The audience already knows that Biff's fall did not result from his failure to pass math, and that it is only Willy who has insisted on that being the defining moment of Biff's life. In reality, it was his refusal to take a summer school course in math that prevented him from graduating and accepting one of the three university offers that he held. The climactic scene of the play explains exactly what happened and exactly why Willy has consistently misrepresented and denied the reality of what did happen.

Young Biff goes to Boston because he feels he has let his father down and because he is totally confident that his father can use his personality on Mr. Birnbaum to get the teacher to change his mind. He tells Willy, "if he saw the kind of man you are, and you just talked to him in your way, I'm sure he'd come through for me." Biff's faith in the persona that his father has projected remains absolute: he still believes that personality and initiative are a more effective route to success than application and study. However, when The Woman appears from the bathroom, Biff instantly realizes that the image he has been taught to admire is "phony." Willy lies to him about no one being in the bathroom and then lies about The Woman's room being painted – they are not even good lies. When the lies collapse, Willy virtually throws "Miss Francis" out, though not before she reminds him that he "promised me stockings, Willy." When she has gone, Willy doubles down on his lie claiming that she is a buyer who "sees merchandise in her room," which accounts for why it is being painted – another transparent lie. Everything Willy has said to Biff appears likewise to be fake: his tales of his success in making sales, his predictions of owning his own business, his guidance about how to succeed. Biff no longer wants or seeks his father's approval; he no longer believes in his father's power to influence Mr. Birnbaum.

Willy's supposed devotion to Linda is also revealed to be false: Willy cheats on his wife sexually and materially, for while Linda darns stockings at home, he gives stockings to his mistress. Desperately, Willy seeks Biff's understanding of his infidelity, but Biff refuses, shouting at him, "You fake! You phony little fake!"

However, Biff not only rejects his father as an individual, he also rejects Willy's version of the American Dream: Biff no longer *wants* to succeed in the world of business even if he could. This explains a crucial misunderstanding by Willy of his son's subsequent motivation. Willy needs to believe that Biff, having lost respect for him as a father, gave up on his belief that *he* could achieve the American Dream. This is what Willy means when he says that Biff failed in order to spite him because Biff knew how important his success was to Willy. This is not, however, what happened. Although he would not realize it until the moment he caught himself running down a flight of stairs with Bill Oliver's pen in his hand, the incident in Boston destroyed Biff's belief in his father's version of the American Dream; that is, Biff no longer *wanted* to spend his life in the corporate world *even if* he could have been successful in it. Biff rejected Willy's conception of urban prosperity, though it would be fifteen years before he found anything to put in its place.

Although it probably makes no impression on Biff at the time, an important feature of Willy's character is the disgracefully unfeeling way in which he treats "Miss Francis." At the start, The Woman comments that he is "the saddest, self-centeredest soul I ever see-saw," and the rest of the scene validates this. When the knocking is first heard, Willy simply gives her orders, as though he can deny reality through force of his personality, treating her in much the same way as we have seen him treat Linda. Once Biff sees her, Willy's only concern is with his own reputation in his son's eyes. He shows no concern or any feelings for The Woman, at one point trying physically to bundle her into the hall before she has dressed. When she reminds him, quite forcefully, of the promised stockings, he first says "I have no stockings here!" and then immediately backs down by giving her the stockings. Not only is this a bribe to get her to go, it suggests that the entire nature of their affair is mercenary rather than emotional or romantic. Having achieved his end in getting rid of her, Willy continues to lie about "Miss Francis." His sole concern throughout the entire scene is himself.

Real Time in Frank's Chop House ("Willy: I gave you an order…" to "Well, whatta you looking at?")

135. Willy gives Stanley money and tells him, "I don't need it anymore." Shortly afterwards, Willy says (speaking to no one in particular), "I've got to get some seeds right away. Nothing's planted. I don't have a thing in the ground." How are these (apparently) unconnected ideas inextricably linked in Willy's mind? (To put it another way: Why *doesn't* Willy need money and why *does* he need to plant seeds? What action is he contemplating? How do you know?)

Commentary

Stanley enters because Willy's shouting is creating a disturbance in the restaurant. He is considerate and concerned, like a surrogate son to a man whose real sons have just abandoned him. Picking up on this, Willy tips him extravagantly, briefly reliving his image of himself as the patriarchal provider. He tells Stanley, "I don't need it [money] any more." Harold Bloom explains Willy's state of mind in this way, "Willy makes meaning by choosing between two ideals which he cannot make compatible: he gives away his money and goes in search of seeds" (*Guides* 63). If this is true, it must be added that Willy retains faith in the dream of success in business, if not for himself, then for his favorite son. Willy has decided to kill himself in order to get the insurance money for Biff as a way of making up to him for what happened in Boston and thus clearing the way for Biff to fulfill the hopes that Willy has personally abandoned.

Willy asks about a seed store. He desires to leave behind him some tangible proof a having lived a successful life; the growing of vegetables will redeem Willy's failure to 'cultivate' Biff properly. It also speaks to his inherent love of nature. However, Stanley comments "it may be too late now." This is true in every sense except the one in which he intends it, for Willy does succeed in finding a store that is still open. It is too late, however, for him to plant something, to get something "in the ground" for his urban dream of making it in business has cut Willy off from his rural heritage. The city has encroached on the green space around the Loman house, cutting off the light and making the ground infertile. It is too late to give Biff the legacy he needs to get a start in the business world, because Biff has finally discovered the kind of life that he *wants* to live, not to spite his father but to give *himself* contentment.

Although Happy has not seen that his father's vision is "phony," it is too late for Willy to regain his love and admiration because Happy sees his father as personally lacking the skills necessary to achieve success. To Happy, Willy is not a "phony" but he has been a failure.

Real Time in the Loman House a Few Hours Later ("Happy: Hey, what're you doing up?" to "Biff: ... Pop!")

136. By reference to the sons' opening dialogue with their mother, illustrate the fact that Happy has not changed at all since the start of the play while Biff has changed radically.

137. As he plants seeds in the garden, Willy mumbles, "What a proposition, ts, ts. Terrific, terrific." Explain the "proposition" he has in mind and what is important about his use of that word to describe it. Speaking to Ben he says, "I see it like a diamond, shining in the dark, hard and rough, that I can pick up and touch in my hand." What exactly is the "it" to which he is referring? Why does he make the comparison with "a diamond"? Is that a valid comparison?

138. How does Willy's description of his own funeral and the impact that it will have on Biff show that he (like Happy) has not changed at all since the start of the play?

139. Biff tells Willy, "To hell with whose fault it is or anything like that." This is a surprising thing for Biff to say given his attitude in the play up to his meeting with Oliver. What has he realized about the incident in Boston in relation to the wider issues of the life-choices that he has made and knows that he must make in the future?

140. Why does Biff at first take all the blame for his failure? Why does he then change insisting, "The man don't know who we are! The man is gonna know! *To Willy:* We never told the truth for ten minutes in this house"?

141. When Biff stopped running down the stairs from Bill Oliver's office was the precise moment of his epiphany. What does the pen come to symbolize for Biff in that moment? How does understanding that symbolism help Biff?

142. Biff's attempts to explain what he has learned about himself (and, of course, about Willy and Happy) completely fail. Explain the reasons why.

143. Finally, an exhausted Biff cries. Comment on the reactions of Linda and of Happy to his tears. Explain the tragic ironies in the following statements:
- the conclusion that Willy draws from Biff's tears, "That boy – that boy is going to be magnificent!";
- Linda's comment, "It's all settled now";
- Happy's promise, "I'm getting married ... I'm changing everything. I'm gonna run that department before the year is up";
- Linda's statement. "I think this is the only way, Willy";
- Willy's assertion, "Ben, he'll worship me for it."

Commentary

When Linda is not in a position where she feels that she has to be subservient to Willy, protecting him by supporting his illusions, she can be assertive, as she is now. In many ways, the ending of Act II parallels the ending of Act I in this respect, but the difference is that there are no more stories to tell that will allow Willy to hope. Linda knows that what has happened at the restaurant has decisively tipped the balance of her husband's mind – the evidence is before her in his futile attempts to plant seeds in the dark. Linda feels that Biff and Happy, who promised to save Willy by giving him something for which to hope, have betrayed their father.

Faced with his mother's accusations, Happy simply lies, telling her that Willy, "had a swell time with us. Listen when I – ... desert him I hope I don't outlive the day!" The problem here is not just that Happy is lying, but that he actually *believes* what he is saying. However, when Happy claims, "He had a great time with us –" Biff cuts him off. Unlike his brother, Biff accepts every insult that his mother throws at him. Biff now knows who he is, and he is determined that Willy will also know, telling Linda, "We're gonna have an abrupt conversation, him and me." Typically, Linda tries to protect Willy from hearing disturbing truths, first by forbidding Biff from seeing his father and then by begging him not to do so. She fails.

Planting his garden, Willy repeats the credo that has motivated him all his life, "A man can't go out the way he came in ... a man has got to add up to something" – that is why he is planting seeds that will germinate after he is dead: they will be his legacy. Willy imagines himself talking to Ben about the $20,000 proposition, the one big business deal he will make in his life. For the first time, there is no element of memory in Willy's imaginative creation, making it clear that "Ben" represents a part of Willy consciousness. He uses the persona 'Ben' to argue the pros and cons of suicide. Initially, Ben is cautious warning that the insurance company may not pay up and that Biff will despise his father for killing himself. However, Willy ignores these warnings, without actually answering them. At last Willy feels that he will have, as Ben says, "something one can feel with the hand." It is the closest Willy can come to "a diamond, shining in the dark, hard and rough, that I can pick up and touch with my hand"; it will be the equivalent of Ben walking into the dark jungle and walking out a rich man; it will be a heroic act of courage. In this way, it will be different from all of the failed "damned-fool appointments" on which he has previously pinned his hopes.

Harold Bloom concludes, "In Ben's presence Willy imagines death as a kind of pioneering journey into the dark wilderness where his insurance money will turn into diamonds and both his and Biff's life are redeemed" (*Guides* 65). However, Willy is *still* deluding himself with his old dream of having personality and being well liked. Recalling the funeral 'of Dave Singleman, he predicts that his own "funeral will be massive!" All of the other salesmen and buyers will come convincing Biff "once and for all" that his father was somebody. Suicide will vindicate Willy's own decision to seek his fortune in selling.

William Arnes points to the significance of Miller's juxtaposition of Willy's decision-making and his planting, "because the garden planting leads to nothing, it becomes an ironic commentary on the suicide Willy considers as he plants the garden. Still caught, even while acknowledging failure, in his need to succeed, Willy plots yet one more action that will bear fruit, prove his worth, and show that his life had meaning. But … Willy's suicide, like the garden he plants, does not bear fruit" (Bloom ed. *Interpretations* 100).

Biff interrupts Willy's imaginary discussion with Ben. Having failed in the restaurant to make Willy understand that "Today I realized something about myself," Biff simply proposes to leave – for once without an argument. It is Willy who makes this impossible by clinging to the false narrative of Biff's meeting with Oliver. Given that, in Willy's mind, Oliver greeted Biff affectionately, the only explanation for Biff refusing to go to the lunch meeting is spite – his son's desire to get back at Willy for the hurt that Willy caused him in Boston. Willy insists, "I want you to know … that you cut down your life for spite!" Willy is so concerned to avoid being blamed for Biff's failure that he fails to recognize that, as Biff insists, he is *not* blaming Willy.

By putting the rubber hose on the table, Biff is bringing the truth to light in a way that Willy can no longer ignore. Typically, both Happy and Linda, who seek to obfuscate reality, are appalled. Finally, Biff insists that Willy is "gonna hear the truth – what you are and what I am!" and Happy and Linda, co-conspirators in maintaining Will's fantasies at all costs, are also going to hear. First, he strips Happy of his lie about his position; then he strips himself by admitting that he was in jail for theft in Kanasa City. Willy again denies responsibility, but Biff insists that his father *was* responsible, *not* because of what happened in Boston, but *because*, "you blew me so full of hot air I never could stand taking orders from anybody! … I had to be boss big shot in two weeks…" This, Biff insists, was Willy's fault: the way he brought him up. Biff needs his father to free him from the weight of his expectation so that he can be himself. To accept this would mean Willy abandoning his illusions about himself and admitting that he is just like everyone else. Even though, deep down, he knows that he has failed his family, Willy cannot do that.

Biff describes the moment of epiphany earlier in the day when he suddenly realized who he was. It began with a view of the sky – the same sky Willy has been trying to see through the high-rise blocks throughout the play. The pen becomes for Biff a symbol of the success in business that Willy has taught him to want and that he now realizes he has never really wanted. He tells Willy, "all I want is out there, waiting for me the minute I say I know who I am!" Biff has realized that he is nothing special and he needs his father to understand that "You were never anything but a hard-working drummer who landed in the ash like all the rest of them!" Willy still insists that Biff is saying this out of spite, but Biff denies it. He desperately wants to save his father from the same delusion that has almost ruined his own life. Crying, he begs Willy to "take that phony dream and burn it before something happens." It is the dream that Biff hates; he does not hate his father, the dreamer. But does he love his father, as Linda asserts; does he even *like* his father as Willy concludes? Critics have generally accepted Linda's and Willy's assertions at face value, but there is little in the text to support either view. Phelps concludes that "If Biff indeed does not love his father, Willy's suicide must be regarded as just the last in the series of futile, misguided gestures that made up his life" (Learner and Learner ed. 76).

Tragically, Willy misunderstands what he has just experienced. He understands that spite is *not* preventing Biff's progress and believes that Biff *loves* him, but draws from this the conclusion that he, Willy, has one final opportunity to achieve success; in doing so, he ignores what Biff has explained about why he no longer *wants* to succeed in, even to live in, the urban business world. (He is also ignoring the objections that Ben made earlier.) As a result, Willy draws entirely the wrong conclusion, shouting out, "That boy – that boy is going to be magnificent!" Willy will kill himself in a final act of deluded self-vindication. The salesman will sell the only thing he has left, his own life, to give Biff the one thing that he neither needs nor wants: $20,000 to start a business.

Unlike Biff, Happy remains mired in the "phony dream" repeating his promise to get married and vowing, "I'm changing everything. I'm gonna run that department before the year is up." None of that will happen: Happy has learned nothing. Linda similarly acquiesces in illusions that paper over the cracks, telling Happy, "You're both good boys, just act that way, that's all." She knows better.

When Linda says "this is the only way, Willy," she means letting Biff go to live his own life, but when Willy replies, "Sure, it's the best way," he is referring to his plan to provide Biff with start-up capital. Having understood that Biff does not hate him for Boston, but has always loved him *despite* Boston, Willy absurdly believes, "he'll worship me for it!" because he will have put his son, "ahead of Bernard again." Willy's error is to repeat the action of his own father and his brother who each walked out on Willy and his mother in their search for wealth. Similarly, Willy chooses suicide, abandoning his own family in order to get the payout of his life insurance. To Willy, money is still the only measure of success: being a loving, hard-working husband and father has never been enough.

REQUIEM

144. What cannot Linda understand about the funeral?
145. Explain why Willy's suicide is to her an inexplicable action.
146. What is Charley trying to explain when he says, "No man needs a little salary"?
148. Who is right: Biff, who says of Willy, "He never knew who he was"; or Charley who tells Biff, "You don't understand ... A salesman is got to dream, boy. It comes with the territory"; or Happy who says, "He had a good dream. It's the only dream you can have – to come out number-one man"? Explain your answer.
149. Analyze the different levels of meaning of the closing words of Linda's final speech, "We're free and clear ... We're free ... We're free ... We're free ..."

Commentary

Only Willy's wife, his two sons, Charley and Bernard attend the funeral; none of his customers or colleagues come – not even Howard Wagner. Rather than illustrate to his sons how "well-liked" he was, the funeral is testimony to how unremarkable Willy was. The tragic irony is that, Linda having made the last payment of their mortgage, the Lomans have finally attained financial security. Having worked for thirty-five years, Willy has committed suicide days before he and Linda could enjoy the results of his labor. He dies unreconciled to Biff, whom he still misunderstands, and a dangerously false role model to Happy, who continues to misinterpret his father.

This little scene has received a fair amount of criticism. Somehow, it just does not seem to fit with the play we have just seen. Ruby Cohn argues that it "violates" the form of the play because it is the only entire scene which is (since Willy is dead) "jarringly and flagrantly outside" Willy's mind. If the contributions of Happy and Biff are clearly consistent with the presentation of their characters in Acts One and Two, many critics have found the (much longer and more impactful) speeches of Charley and Linda to be inconsistent with the characters we have come to know, for example, in the elevated language that each uses here but also in the perspective on Willy's life and death that they give here. Edward Murray explains why he finds Requiem unsatisfactory:

> Technically ... it violates the convention of point of view, and, although it helps to focus the theme, it says nothing really new, nothing that has not been better expressed in the previous action. Moreover, in its final utterance, it is even somewhat specious and confusing. (Siebold ed. *Salesman* 35-36)

William Aarnes observes the same lack of clarity in what the characters say about Willy, but finds it to be deliberate on Miller's part:

> [T]he play's final scene continues the debunking of Willy ... [R]ather than clarifying Willy's life, the statements of the characters at Willy's graveside serve only to demonstrate that they are simply too confused by Willy's life to deal with it honestly and meaningfully ... [T]hey are all incapable of seeing meaning in Willy's life ... [A]ny suggestion that the characters grouped around the grave make up a chorus is ironic. Not only do these characters fail to speak together as one group that has arrived at an agreed-upon conclusion about the meaning of Willy's life, but, in failing to understand even each other, they also come near to failing to speak to one another. They are separate people, and the Lomans are no longer, if they ever were, a family. (Bloom ed. *Interpretations* 104-106)

Miller has been accused of speaking through Charley to establish the dignity of Willy's character and the universality of his tragic fate. Having spent the entire play urging Willy to be a pragmatist like himself, Charley waxes sentimental, presenting his dream not as something that he could (and should) cast aside but as something that comes with the territory of every salesman. Linda does not understand why "all the people he knew" stayed away, suggesting that (despite her more realistic approach to life) she bought into Willy's illusions about himself, yet she has heard for years that people simply do not take to Willy and more recently that the buyers with whom he did do business have either retired or died. More fundamentally, she cannot understand her husband killing himself (despite having found the rubber tubing near the gas jet and having read the car insurance reports on Willy's 'accidents') at a time when they are, after thirty-five years, financially "free and clear." She apparently has never understood that Willy wanted more than a modest middle class life, which is all that she herself wanted. As Ruby Cohn writes, "it is difficult to understand her lack of understanding" (Bloom ed. *Interpretations* 45).

More consistently, Happy and Biff interpret Willy's suicide in terms of their own perspective on his business dreams: Happy plans to stay in New York and succeed where his father failed, while Biff rejects the business ethos that destroyed his father and plans to live in the country. Happy blames his father's weaknesses for his personal failure, but he still believes in Willy's dreams. Biff, however, knows the truth: there was more of Willy Loman in the front stoop that he built than "in all the sales he ever made." In a tragedy, there comes a point when the tragic hero understands his/her error. It is the point when Othello, realizing that Iago has manipulated him into killing his innocent wife, Desdemona, cries out, "O fool! fool! fool!" (5.2). Willy never reaches that point, *but Biff has*. Now he says firmly that Willy, "had the wrong dreams. All,

all, wrong ... He never knew who he was." Typically Happy responds, "Don't say that!" – the truth must still be avoided at all costs.

Charley, Willy's only friend, delivers a eulogy on the nature of a salesman's dreams rendered in an anachronistic, pseudo-spiritual language ("Nobody dast blame this man"). Charley tries to explain to Linda that, "No man only needs a little salary," and he should know because, after all, he has repeatedly been offering Willy $50 a week only to be rejected. Charley understands that a man's pride necessitates that he have belief in being able to provide more than the basics; a man needs to believe he is building something, not just getting by. Charley claims that it is Biff who does not understand: he does not understand that a salesman (unlike a tradesman, a lawyer or a doctor) has nothing to rely upon except his own self-image, which makes a salesman uniquely vulnerable. That's why "A salesman is got to dream..." Charley gives Willy's quest for self-validation a significance in spiritual terms that makes his suicide explicable if not excusable. Whether the Charley who appears in the first two acts would, or even could, make such a speech is, as explained above, open to question.

Biff remains unconvinced: Willy was a man who should have been an artisan living in the outdoors making money by using his manual skills. That is the life that Biff intends to follow, and he invites Happy to join him. Happy, however, is determined to stay in the city and "beat this racket." (Notice that Happy speaks in clichés.) In turn, he asks Biff to join him, and in turn, Biff refuses. Happy asserts his belief in "the only dream you can have [is] – to come out number-one man." Willy may have failed, but Happy affirms that he will not, and that by succeeding he will prove that "Willy Loman did not die in vain." Biff knows that there is no more point arguing with his brother than there was arguing with his father.

Linda is the only one of the three characters to speak who admits to not understanding her husband. For Linda, owning a home, having a range of modern appliances, raising a family and having a husband who worked for the same firm for thirty-five years was enough, and she does not understand why it was not enough for Willy. Once again, it is an open question whether the Linda of the first two acts would, or could, have spoken as she does here.

Willy might have echoed the final words of Nick Carraway at the conclusion of *The Great Gatsby* by F. Scott Fitzgerald when he is trying to relate Gatsby's impossible quest for a lost, perfect love to the struggles that all humans make *because* they are human. He writes:

> Gatsby believed in the green light, the orgastic future that year by year recedes before us. It eluded us then, but that's no matter – tomorrow we will run faster, stretch out our arms farther ... And then one fine morning –
>
> So we beat on, boats against the current...[1]

If both Gatsby and Willy fall short of being tragic because each dies with his illusions intact, both approach the tragic because of the tenacity with which they hold a dream that gives meaning to their lives.

[1. It is always with mixed feelings that I read in the work of another critic a point that I made on the assumption that it was entirely original: on the positive side, it proves I was on the right track, but on the negative side, I can no longer claim to have made the point first. Bigsby's essay "*Death of a Salesman*: In Memoriam" (Bloom ed. *Interpretations* 113-128) ends with the same point and the same quotation as I used here before I had read it.]

Perspectives

These post-reading questions are ideal for individual reflection, group discussion or written answers.

1. "*Death of a Salesman* is a play written along the lines of the finest classical tragedy. It is the revelation of a man's downfall, in [sic] destruction whose roots are entirely in his own soul. The play builds to an immutable conflict where there is no resolution for this man in this life." (Hawkins "*Death of a Salesman* Powerful Tragedy," Weales ed. 202)

2. "[Its] hero, the desperate salesman Willy Loman, is too much the loud-mouth dolt and emotional babe-in-the-woods to wear all the trappings of high tragedy with which he has been invested." (John Grassner "*Death of a Salesman*: First Impressions, 1949," Weales ed. 232)

3. Critics have occasionally claimed that *Salesman* is not a particularly 'well-made' play. Here is a compendium of the faults that have been suggested:

- Biff claims to have stolen a carton of basketballs from Bill Oliver while he was working for him, but basketballs are rather large items and a whole carton of them would be difficult to hid;
- Happy says that manufacturers occasionally offer him $100 to direct an order to them, but given his assistant of the assistant position, it seems unlikely that he would have the power to do this;
- Given the report of the insurance inspector on Willy's previous car accidents, it seems inconceivable that the insurance company would pay $20,000 following Willy's death in a car accident.

Can you think of any other pieces of the play that just do not quite 'fit'? Are such details of any importance to you in your evaluation of the play?

4. "*Death of a Salesman* may be an important play; it may be a historically significant play; it is not, however, a good play." Do you agree?

5. Examine the view that the only character worthy to be considered the play's protagonist is Biff.

6. Would the play be better without Requiem?

7. "Too many of the characters in the play simply do not come to life. Charley and Bernard are worthy but dull; Howard is a caricature; The Woman lacks all substance; Linda lacks consistency; Happy has no depth. The conflict between Biff and Willy is not enough to hold our interest." Do you agree?

8. Outline what you think will happen to Linda, Happy and Biff in the next ten years.

Critical Analysis
Dramatis Personae: Introduction to the Significant Characters
The Loman Family:
Willy Loman is the play's protagonist. Born in 1886, he is sixty-three and has been a travelling salesman representing the Wagner firm in New England for almost thirty-six years. (The play never indicates what it is that the company produces.) Although he tells his wife Linda, "When I went north the first time, the Wagner Company didn't know where New England was!" and claims that he is still "the New England man ... vital in New England," it becomes clear as the play progresses that Willy has never been a particularly successful salesman, and that in recent years his productivity has fallen significantly as his old contacts have retired or died. Five weeks before the start of the play, Willy's boss, Howard Wagner, took him off salary and put him on straight commission. He has hidden this fact from Linda, his wife (although she knows), and made up the loss of income by borrowing $50 a week from his friend and neighbor Charley.

The play opens late on a Monday evening. Early that morning, Willy had set off to drive from Brooklyn, where he lives, to Portland, Maine, where he has an appointment on Tuesday morning to show the Wagner line to representatives of Brown and Morrison (presumably a retail store). However, Willy has turned back because he found his concentration wandering. He tells Linda, "all of a sudden I'm going off the road! ... I absolutely forgot I was driving," and with even more honesty, he admits to his son Happy, "I got an awful scare. Nearly hit a kid in Yonkers." We learn that, over the last year, Willy has had a number of car accidents which the insurance inspector decided were *not* accidents at all. A witness at one of these crashes stated, "he came to that little bridge, and then deliberately smashed into the railing, and it was only the shallowness of the water that saved him." Linda is convinced that Willy has been trying to kill himself because she has also found rubber tubing in the basement that Willy could hook up to the gas pipe.

Willy is evidently in the advanced stages of a complete nervous breakdown (today we might call it 'dementia'), because his dream of success is finally disintegrating before the reality of his failure as a salesman, as a husband and as a father. It is not only the reality of his failing career that is on Willy's mind. It becomes clear that he and his eldest son Biff, who were once very close, have been estranged for the last fifteen years. The complex reasons for this estrangement become clear as the play progresses.

Linda Loman is Willy's unwaveringly loving and supportive wife. Despite the fact that Willy frequently treats her rudely and dismissively, she not only loves him but respects him, and feels deeply the injustice of the way he is being treated by the firm he has worked for so long. She tells her sons, "A small man can be just as exhausted as a great man," and that "there's more good in him than in many other people."

Knowing that the only thing that keeps Willy going are his dreams, she often encourages him to believe in his ability to achieve success despite the fact that she knows from experience the reality of his inevitable failure. She tells her sons, "It takes so little to make him happy," and she is prepared to do whatever it takes to make him hopeful about the future. At the same time, she has no illusions about the reality of their financial situation and works tirelessly to make ends meet.

Linda has dedicated her life to keeping the family going and the strain of doing so has made her prematurely old. During the course of the play, she has three aims: to keep Willy from committing suicide; to heal the rift between Willy and Biff (the cause of which she does not know); and to make Happy into a more responsible son. To achieve her aims, Linda is not afraid to confront both Biff and Happy about their poor treatment of their father and with the seriousness of his mental condition, but she does not show the same willingness to confront Willy with the truth because she fears it would tip him over the edge.

Biff Loman is the elder of the two Loman boys; born in 1915, he is thirty-four years old. Throughout his childhood, Biff idolized his father and was, in turn, Willy's favorite. In 1932, as a senior in high school, he was the star quarterback of the football team, and in his final year he had offers of scholarships from three universities, including the University of Virginia. All of the boys looked up to him, and he was very popular with the girls. Biff seemed destined for great success in the business world having absorbed all of the advice Willy gave him. However, in the Regents examination, Biff failed math, which meant that he did not have enough credits to graduate. This should have been no more than a minor set-back, but Biff never did retake math and so never graduated. The reason for this becomes clear as the play progresses.

After high school, Biff went to work for a local firm, but he was impatient for success and compensated by stealing from his employer which got him sacked. Since then, Biff's stealing has got him fired from a whole string of jobs. Eventually, sometime around 1934, he moved away from New York and has most recently been working on a ranch in Texas; part of him likes the work, but part of him is dissatisfied because on what he earns he knows he will never amount to anything, which is the goal that Willy drummed into him.

As the play starts, Biff is on one of his infrequent visits home. Neither he nor his father has told either Linda or Happy the reason for their mutual antagonism. Willy blames Biff for failing to live up to his potential in the business world, and Biff sees Willy as a "phony" – a failure trying to maintain the illusion that he is a success. Whenever they are together, they quarrel; nevertheless, Biff has a great deal of love for his father.

Happy Loman is Biff's thirty-two-year-old brother. Throughout their childhood, Happy lived in Biff's shadow, never being able to compete with him in athletic achievement or in popularity with his peers. Above all, however, Happy has always known that his father favored Biff. After high school, he got a job in the city, and he is currently an assistant to an assistant buyer in a department store. On a salary of seventy dollars a week, he has hardly climbed the corporate ladder, and as he tells Biff, "I don't know what the hell I'm workin' for … It's what I always wanted. My own apartment, a car, and plenty of women. And still, goddammit, I'm lonely." Having put Willy's values and dreams into practice, he has seen them fail both in terms of his inability to gain promotion and the failure of materialism to bring contentment. Unfortunately, this is a truth that Happy is reluctant to face.

Like his brother, Happy compensates for his lack of success and his thwarted professional ambition by stealing. In his case, he seduces the girlfriends of his superiors and takes the occasional bribe because, as he tells Biff, "Manufacturers offer me a hundred-dollar bill now and then to throw an order their way."

Willy's Father is, of course, long dead by the time in which the play is set. Everything we learn about him comes from Willy's brother Ben during one of Willy's imaginative recreations of the past and must therefore be treated as unreliable. Ben describes their father as "a very great and a very wild-hearted man" constantly on the move with his family in a covered wagon. Among other things, he made and sold flutes, but he also was a "Great inventor" who with one "gadget … made more than a man like you [Willy] could make in a lifetime." All that Willy remembers of his father is "a man with a big beard" because, in c.1889, he seems to have suddenly abandoned his wife and two sons to seek his fortune in Alaska. Nothing is recorded of his fate there.

Willy is extremely proud of his father, but it is his heroic pursuit of wealth than attracts him more than his skills as a craftsman. The main difference between father and son is that the former produced by his own hands the products he sold, whereas Willy is a salesman in the age of mass production; he sells products manufactured by machines tended by production-line workers. Only in his leisure time is Willy able to use the making skills he inherited from his father.

Willy's Mother is a shadowy, insubstantial figure who looked after Ben and Willy after being deserted by her husband and then looked after Willy when Ben set out to find his father. Willy seems to have kept in touch with her, but she has been dead for many years.

Willy's Brother Ben is Willy's wealthy older brother who has recently died (apparently without leaving to Willy any of the vast fortune he is supposed to have accumulated). Since Ben appears only in Willy's memories of his two visits to Brooklyn, it is difficult to separate truth from fiction, that is, to separate the real Ben from Willy's desperate need to see Ben as a symbol of the success that he desperately craves for himself and for his sons. To Willy, Ben is "the only man I ever met who knew the answers," though his efforts to get Ben to explain those answers never come to anything.

Ben claims that he left Willy and their mother in South Dakota in order to find their father who had abandoned the family earlier to go to Alaska. Willy tells him that as a child, "I remember you walking down some open road." Ben's "very faulty view of geography," however, took him to Africa. He boasts to Biff and Happy, "Why boys, when I was seventeen I walked into the jungle, and when I was twenty-one, I walked out … And by God I was rich." Quite how Ben became rich is unclear, as is Willy's memory that on one of his visits Ben asked him to go with him to Alaska because, "Opportunity is tremendous in Alaska."

Charley's Family

Charley is Willy's next-door neighbor and his oldest (and only remaining) friend. He owns a successful business (although we never learn what that business is). Aware of the real problems Willy is having to face, Charley gives Willy money to pay his bills and is constantly offering to give his friend a job in his firm. However, Willy resents Charley's success and is always too proud to accept the offer of a job since to do so would be an admission of his own failure. Charley shows great patience in trying to help Willy without offending him, but doing so places great psychological strain on him.

Bernard is Charley's son. At high school he was in the same year as Biff; he was a good student who hero-worshipped Biff. He was always encouraging him to study, particularly math, and offering to help him. Willy used to mock Bernard for studying hard, calling him "an anemic" and asking his boys rhetorically, "Bernard is not well liked, is he?" However, Bernard turned out to be right about Biff's math teacher, Mr. Birnbaum, failing him, and at the time of the play he has become a successful lawyer who is just about to argue a case before the Supreme Court. It is difficult for Willy to accept that Bernard has been successful in the business world while his own sons have so conspicuously failed since he sees Bernard as lacking in personality and drive which are for Willy the prerequisites of success.

Since our only source for what Bernard was like as a teenager is Willy's memories, it is entirely possible that he was never quite as "anemic" as he appears to have been in the high school scenes. Bernard reports that, when Biff returned from Boston, the two of them "had a fist fight. It lasted for at least half an hour. Just the two of us, punching each other down the cellar, and crying right through it." This certainly suggests that Bernard was more robust than he appears to be in Willy's memories of him, a view which is also more consistent with the exceptional success he has achieved in his chosen profession and his enthusiasm for playing tennis.

The Wagner Family

Frank Wagner (Old Man Wagner) was the man for whom Willy worked most of the years he spent with the company. Willy still regards him as "a masterful man" and "a prince." In Willy's memories his old boss respected him and, in recognition of his outstanding sales, made certain verbal promises about Willy's future with the company. As Willy remembers him, Frank is one of the last representatives of a previous age in business when honor, friendship and relationships were still important – the age in which Dave Singleman lived.

Howard Wagner is Willy's current boss. Howard inherited the company from his father, but (at least in Willy's mind) he has a very different business philosophy. To Howard, business decisions are dependent upon the bottom line – which means profit. Howard is under no illusion that Willy was ever an outstanding salesman and has seen his productivity fall in the last few years. Despite this, and a number of sales trips aborted due to car accidents, he has kept Willy employed, even to the extent of taking him off salary but letting him work on commission only. This can only be because Howard feels a sense of loyalty to Willy, perhaps for his father's sake. However, the cancelled trip to Portland spurs Howard to fire Willy, an action he has been wanting to take for some time. Evidently Howard is more compassionate than his insistence that "business is business" would suggest.

Other Characters

Mr. Birnbaum, a high school math teacher, never appears in the play, but has a key role in Biff's development. Presumably in an effort to get Biff to buckle down and actually do some work (or at least to turn up to class regularly), he makes it quite clear that he will give Biff a fail grade in his Math if he does not make the grade. Predictably, Biff ignores the warnings, and Birnbaum keeps his word.

The Woman was Willy's mistress in Boston when Happy and Biff were in high school. She is never named, though when Biff finds the two of them together Willy calls her "Miss Francis." The Woman is a secretary for one of Willy's buyers. She tells Willy that she is attracted to him because of his "sense of humor" and the fact that they "have such a good time together." To Willy, who gets lonely on the road and depressed by his modest sales, her admiration is a necessary boost to his fragile ego. The Woman is the only character who actually buys into Willy's image of himself, though it is worth remembering that the only things we learn about her we get from Willy's distorting memories.

Biff goes to Boston to see his father after Mr. Birnbaum gives him a fail for his math class. Arriving unannounced, he catches Willy in his hotel room with

The Woman. At this moment, he loses faith in his father and in his father's dream of making a success in the business world – both seem to him to be irredeemably phony. Although Biff never tells anyone about the encounter in the hotel room, he makes no effort to pass math and gives up on the idea of going to college. Having lost his identity as football hero, scholarship winner and potential business success, he no longer knows who his is or who he wants to be.

Stanley is a waiter at Frank's Chop House who seems to be well acquainted with Happy.

Miss Forsythe and **Letta** are two attractive young women whom Happy and Biff meet at Frank's Chop House. It seems unlikely that Miss Forsythe and Letta are actually prostitutes, but judging from Happy's repeated comments about their moral character, they are "on call."

Jenny is Charley's secretary. She is sympathetic to Willy but incapable of dealing with him.

Settings

Although the action of the play takes place exclusively in urban New York, it is possible to distinguish a number of settings. The West is a vanished frontier than exists only in Willy's shadowy memories of the family travelling with his father in a covered wagon, that iconic symbol of the settler opening up a new land and starting a new life. At the turn of the twentieth century, when Willy was a young man in his prime, Alaska and Africa were the last remaining frontiers, regions rich in mineral wealth, where an individual could still, with a mixture of good luck and ruthless exploitation, strike it rich. They were the last remaining undeveloped regions in the world – the last places where the pioneering spirit that drove people to find a new life in the American West was still applicable. In contrast, New England, still represents traditional American culture. It was the cradle of the Revolution that balances the natural beauty of its countryside with the enterprise of its beautiful trading cities. New York represents the city of the mid-twentieth century, expanding unstoppably into the suburbs. New York is without natural beauty; it is a place of competition where human values no longer operate. Its epitome is the chop house. De Schweinitz writes, "The scene in the restaurant … comes closer to a picture of Hell than any other piece of modern literature…" (Weales ed. 278).

In the chronology of the play's settings we see a changing relationship between man and his environment. The myth of Grandfather Loman, constructed by his sons, is of a man at one with his environment, "a creative figure, moving in harmony with nature by making and disseminating music," whereas "Ben is an exploiter and despoiler of nature" (Stanton, Bloom ed. *Loman* 129). Willy and Biff share their father's love of the natural world, and have something of their father and Ben's desire to shape the natural world to their own needs with their own hands. Both are trapped, however, by the encroaching city which literally blocks out the light to the Brooklyn house so that nothing grows in the garden any more. Alienated and deeply unhappy in the world of the city, neither Willy nor Biff has had the courage, individualism, nor selfishness simply to walk away from a way of life that they hate. Matthew Roudané brilliantly sums up the decision that Willy makes, "Willy completes the brutalization process [of his experience of business in the city] by reducing himself to a commodity, an object, a thing, which enables him to make the greatest and last sale of his entire professional life: the sale of his very existence for the insurance payment" (Bigsby ed. 80-81).

Genre

Tragedy

In his Introduction to the Viking Critical Library edition of *Death of a Salesman*, Gerald Weales writes, rather wearily, "I cannot avoid the obvious fact that the question most often asked about the play is: is it or isn't it a tragedy?" Despite the fact that Weales asserts that it is a question that "interests me not at all," he concedes that it is a question which has continued to fascinate the play's critics (xiii).

Thus, at the outset, we might ask another question: Why does it *matter* whether *Death of a Salesman* is a tragedy or not? In answer, we may state that whether we class the play as a tragedy or not does not have any relevance to deciding on the play's quality as drama. It is true that some critics take tragedy to be the highest expression of drama, but there are many plays that must be called tragedies but are not very good plays. Really the only reason that it matters whether we call the play a tragedy is that by examining *Salesman* in relation to the concept of tragedy we come better to understand what the play *does* and what it *does not* do. Having understood the play, we will be in a better position to judge its qualities and its defects.

In his essay "Tragedy and the Common Man," published just two weeks after the opening night of *Salesman* (February 10th, 1949), Miller states, "I believe that the common man is as apt a subject for tragedy in its highest sense as kings were" (Weales ed. 143). He argues that, "As a general rule ... the tragic feeling is evoked in us when we are in the presence of a character who is ready to lay down his life, if need be, to secure one thing – his sense of personal dignity" (Ibid. 144). In his own mind at least, this justifies Miller in writing about "the tragedy of Willy Loman" ("The 'Salesman' Has a Birthday," Ibid. 150). In support of this viewpoint, Miller elsewhere makes an important distinction between rank and stature. The fall of a person of high rank, Miller concedes, has a wider social impact that the fall of a "corner grocer," but rank is unconnected with a character's "intensity, the human passion to surpass his given bounds, the fanatical insistence upon his self-conceived role" ("Introduction to *Collected Plays*" Weales ed. 165, 166). Tragedy requires of the hero *consciousness*. Miller finds that consciousness in Willy who, by the end of the play, "has achieved a very powerful piece of knowledge, which is that he is loved by his son and has been embraced by him and forgiven" (Ibid. 167).

In Miller's view, Willy is too completely committed to a false idea of success to do anything other than pursue his disastrous dream to the very end. His tragedy is that he feels that he "can prove his existence only by bestowing 'power' on his posterity, a power derived from the sale of his last asset, himself, for the price of his insurance police" (Ibid.). Miller concludes his argument by writing, "That he [Willy] had not the intellectual fluency to verbalize his situation is not the same thing as saying that he lacked awareness, even an overly intensified consciousness that the life he had made was without form and inner meaning" (Ibid. 168).

Aware that the controversy rests on Willy's level of consciousness at the climax of the drama, Harold Bloom suggests a different way of looking at *Salesman* as a tragedy. He argues that the play "is more the tragedy of a family than it is of an individual or of a society" (*Guides* 8). In this view, Willy "does not die the death of a salesman. He dies the death of a father..." (Ibid. 9). This seems to be a very fruitful way of interpreting the tragic aspects of the play.

Social Criticism

Even a reader coming to the play without any knowledge of Arthur Miller's political views would notice that it is deeply critical of certain aspects of modern capitalist culture (aspects that were, perhaps, uniquely American at the time the play was written, but which are now universal amongst developed Western countries). In telling the Lomans' story, Miller is critical of many aspects of consumerism: deceptive advertising, the installment plan, shoddy workmanship, planned obsolescence, mortgages, debt, low wages. etc. He is even more critical of the business world of the mid-twentieth century because, having established the profit motive as supreme, the more human values (honor, loyalty, long service, friendship, etc.) appear to have been abandoned. Having asserted that Willy Loman is in no sense an average American, Miller told Phillip Gelb, "Willy Loman is, I think, a person who embodies in himself some of the most terrible conflicts running though the streets of America today ("Morality and Drama: Interview with Phillip Gelb," Weales ed. 177).

Willy is also alienated from the means of production because he sells that merchandise that he has no hand in producing. Clurman Harold explains:

> To possess himself fully, a man must have an intimate connection with that with which he deals as well as with the person with whom he deals. When the connection is not more than an exchange of commodities, the man himself ceases to be a man, becomes a commodity himself, a spiritual cipher. This is a humanly untenable situation. Since his function precludes a normal human relationship, he substitutes an imitation of himself for the real man. He sells his "personality" ... a mask worn so long that it soon comes to be mistaken, even by the man who wears it, as his real face. (Weales ed. 213).

Thus Willy's mental breakdown is ultimately the result of his alienation from both the means of production and the means of distribution; he is, quite literally, the middle man with no connection to either. Thus, Willy can only work for his paycheck and the only way he can measure his success is by the size of that pay check – not by the quality of the goods, since he had no part in their production, nor in their usefulness to those who purchase them, since he had no part in selling them to the public. As Richard Foster concludes:

> Willy Loman is potentially better than his world in that he has at least incipient values that are better than the world's values. Society's guilt, as it is projected in *Death of a Salesman*, lies in not making available ways for a man like Willy to implement and realize those values, and in dooming him thus to frustration, paralysis, and ultimately destruction as a human being. (Siebold ed. *Salesman* 106-107)

This discussion raises the related question: Is *Death of a Salesman* a communist/socialist/Marxist play? Asking this question is rather like asking the tragedy question discussed above. For some critics, a communist/socialist/Marxist play *cannot* conceivably be a good play. That is, of course, as much nonsense as is the opposite belief that only a communist/socialist/Marxist play *can* conceivably be a good play. However, asking the question about the nature of the play as social criticism *does* help us to understand the play, and having understood it we will be in a better position to judge of its qualities and its defects.

Our analysis must begin by stating that, like many artists in the 1930s and 1940s, Arthur Miller was attracted to the ideas of Karl Marx and to the way in which those ideas *appeared* to be in the process of being put into practice in the Union of Soviet Socialist Republics. Paul Solman records Miller as saying in a 1999 interview, "I object to it [i.e. "dog-eat-dog competitive capitalism"]. But formerly I thought that a socialist solution would resolve some of these problems. The only thing is, is that where we have had a socialist solution, it has raised up innumerable other problems that you stand and pause a bit before you really could go down that road" (Learner and Learner ed. 52).

To equate Miller's attack on certain aspects of modern consumerism and business practice with a wholesale attack on capitalism must rest on an identification of capitalism as a system with American capitalism in the mid-twentieth century. Certainly there are commentators and historians who would make that equation (just as there have been commentators and historians who have equated communism in Russia, China, Cuba, Venezuela, etc. with communism as a system), but most of us would take the view that it is possible to point to faults in any particular socio-economic system without necessarily attacking the theoretical basis of that system. This seems to be what Miller is doing in *Death of a Salesman*, for, as Bigsby points out, "the play's success in virtually all societies ... shows that it is something more than a dramatization of the American dream, its corruptions and coercions" (Bloom ed. *Interpretations* 116). For the best part of seven decades, audiences around the world have experienced a "shock of recognition" when experiencing "Willy's anguished debate with himself and with the world in which he never felt at home" (Ibid).

The argument that he is simply condemning capitalism from a Marxist perspective has to explain the presence in the play of Charley and Bernard. Charley, whom Miller calls the "most decent man in [the play]" ("Introduction to *Collected Plays*" Weales ed. 170), seems to come from the same class as the Lomans (he did, after all, buy a house on the same street as Willy twenty-five years ago), yet Charley has risen to own a business while Willy is still doing the same job he began when he first joined the Wagner Company. The difference obviously does *not* lie in some fatal flaw in the capitalist system but in the different personalities of the two men. Similarly, Bernard has built upon his father's success. He is the first person in his family to go to university, and he gets there through his own efforts working within the public school system. Biff and Happy had exactly the same chances, but they failed through their own misguided efforts. Bernard seems to be the perfect example of the opportunity offered to everyone by the American free market system: he is the product of a meritocracy that allows those with ability and drive to rise irrespective of the class into which they are born.

In his "Introduction to *Collected Plays*," Miller made yet another argument against seeing this play as anti-capitalist. He writes, "A play cannot be equated with a political philosophy ... I do not believe that any work of art can help but be diminished by its adherence at any cost to a political program, including its author's, and not for any other reason than that there is no political program – any more than there is a theory of tragedy – which can encompass the complexities of real life" (Weales ed. 170). *Salesman* may not be as well written as many critics have claimed, and it may evoke emotion from audiences by some bad (or at least indifferent) writing, but it is *not* a bad play because its critic or viewer is anti-communist.

Realism and Expressionism

Salesman is a drama firmly rooted in the lives of Americans during the late 1940s. As Brian Parker points out, its action, "is filled out with a detailed evocation of modern, urban, lower-middle class life: Miller documents a world of arch supports, aspirin, spectacles, subway, [etc.] ... The language too, except in a few places ... is an accurate record of the groping, half-articulate, cliché-ridden inadequacy of ordinary American speech" (Bloom ed. *Interpretations* 26). In this respect, it would be hard to find a drama more realistic (or naturalistic, since the terms are often loosely used as though they were interchangeable) than this one. In order for the audience to identify with Willy's dilemma, it must recognize the Lomans as people struggling with the very ordinary, often quite trivial, challenges of modern life: making the next payment, replacing a fan belt, fixing a newly-installed shower that leaks, etc. In fact, several every-day appliances can be seen by the audience in the Loman house.

Realism only operates, however, in the real-time scenes; the imagined scenes entirely ignore the restrictions of realism – characters, for example, are free to walk through the invisible lines of walls in the structure of the Loman house because these walls are no longer there. It is frequently forgotten that the play has a subtitle, "Certain Private Conversations in Two Acts and A Requiem." Sockley explains, "The entire play is basically a struggle within Willy's mind between his vision of himself and the painful reality of facts intruding upon his 'dream'" (Siebold ed. *Salesman* 103). This is why it is quite wrong to expect consistency between characters as they are presented in the real-time scenes and in the imaginary memory scenes: the former are representations of objective reality, while the latter are representations of how people appear to be as seen through the distorting lens of Willy's consciousness.

Christopher Innes writes, "the naturalistic present merges into expressionistic memory sequences" (Bloom ed. *Interpretations* 61). The term 'expressionist' is often used to describe Miller's dramatic technique in the scenes that represent what is only happening in Willy's head. Weales notes that the characters in the play (especially, but not exclusively the minor characters) are frequently criticized as lacking individuality. They are, it is often argued stereotypes, but he makes this distinction, "If the play belongs … in the tradition of American realism, then those characters may stand out as unreal, stock. If, however, Miller's borrowing of expressionistic techniques allows him to use a type of character when he needs one to make a point, they may be functioning legitimately within a particular scene" (Weales ed. xix-xx).

Expressionism in art describes the representation of the world from the perspective of a suffering protagonist which radically distorts reality for emotional effect. A simple example will clarify: *The Scream* by Edvard Munch (1863-1944) represents not the scream of an identifiable individual walking across a particular bridge but the universal anxiety of modern man. The way in which the subject and the background are rendered reflects this universal anxiety. Similarly, the imagined memory scenes represent Willy Loman's subjective emotions, and they do so through distortion, exaggeration, and fantasy, as Brian Parker explains:

> Miller is not using expressionistic techniques in the way they were used by the German writers in the 1920s, to dramatize abstract forces in politics or economics or history. He is using the techniques solely as a means of revealing the character of Willy Loman, the values Willy holds and, particularly, the way his mind works. (Bloom ed. *Interpretations* 29)

Characterization

Willy Loman

> Willy Loman does not merely suggest or hint that he is at the end of his strength and of his justifications, he is hardly on the stage for five minutes when he says so; he does not gradually imply a deadly conflict with his son ... he is avowedly grappling with that conflict at the outset. The ultimate matter with which the play will close is announced at the outset and is the matter of its every moment from the first. (Miller "Introduction to *Collected Plays*" Weales ed. 157)

Willy is the product both of his nature and his nurture. From his father, he inherits a love of the outdoors, skill with tools, and the capacity to feel tremendous joy and satisfaction from completing a practical project (such as rebuilding the stoop of his house or putting in a new ceiling). This part of Willy would have been happiest being what his father was, an artisan craftsman, or perhaps a jobbing builder. However, there is another side to Willy's conception of his father. Ben tells him that their father was a "great inventor" who with "one gadget" could make more in a week than Willy could make in a lifetime. Given everything we learn about the man, this seems highly improbable, but Willy never questions its truth. Thus, in Willy's mind, the patriarch of the Loman family combines two quite incompatible qualities: he was an itinerant artisan craftsman who made himself wealthy. In this conception lies the reason for Willy's choice of a career in selling and for his failure to achieve the success (financial and social) that he so desperately craves. Yet as Oscar Brockett points out, Willy's "failure in business is important only because it reflects his failure as a father, husband, and human being" (Sieboldy ed. *Miller* 97). We can trace these failures to his upbringing.

Abandoned as a baby by his father and at the age of "[t]hree years and eleven months" by his elder brother Ben, Willy grew up without a father-figure, and this has resulted in a desperate psychological need for approval. Whilst his father and brother emerge (at least in Willy's memories) as "adventurous" men with a strong "streak of self-reliance" who eventually made their fortunes by their own efforts, Willy lacks their self-confidence; they were risk-takers, and he is not. Nevertheless, part of Willy needs to achieve success and to have that success recognized; the American Dream that a man can rise to the top in the business world through personality and pep, seems to offer him a route to the validation that he so desperately needs – it offers the potential for Willy to achieve a level of success even greater than either his father or his brother.

Harold Bloom explains the incompatible ideas about how to live and how to succeed which lead Willy inevitably to failure:

> The salesman's business ethic dictates behavior that would

endanger life on the frontier; the qualifications for survival on the frontier would likely land a businessman in jail; and Willy's own confused notions about winning success by being "likeable" are insufficient for achieving success of any kind. (*Guides* 44)

Thus, Willy is a character fatally divided between two incompatible lifestyles, and what makes him at least a potentially tragic figure is that the audience understands this division of Willy's psyche but Willy himself is blind to it (just as the audience knows from the start of *Oedipus Rex* that Oedipus is the man who killed his father, Laius, and that his wife, Jocasta, is his mother). Leonard Moss draws attention to the fact that the Lomans' favorite verb is 'to make.' He notes that "This verb occurs forty-five times in thirty-three different usages" (e.g. "make money." "make a mark," "make good," etc.) (27). This unconscious word use shows at once the strength of Willy's inheritance from his father of the skills and the need to make something concrete and the way in which he has attempted (disastrously) to apply that inheritance to a world where, as Charley says over Willy's grave, "a salesman don't put a bolt to a nut…"

The deciding influence in Willy's life is his meeting with the drummer (i.e., traveling sales representative) Dave Singleman, a surrogate father whose example convinces him to abandon his plans to "go out with my older brother and try to locate [my father in Alaska]." The achievements of the eighty-four-year-old Singleman (his ability to go into any town and do business with buyers on the phone from his hotel room and the respect people have for him) convinces Willy that his future lies in selling because Singleman's life and death appear to embody a life in which there is "respect, and comradeship, and gratitude." This decision is an error which will ultimately have fatal consequences for Willy. Firstly, it appears not occur to Willy that if Singleman, at age eighty-four, still needs to be on the road, then he cannot have made enough money to retire. Secondly, Willy does not understand that he simply does not have the qualities of personality or the inter-personal skills necessary for success in selling. Finally, Willy never understands that, while Singleman operated in the business environment of the late nineteenth century when the values which Willy identifies *may* have been operative, Willy own career will play out in the increasingly hard-nosed business world of the twentieth century. As Michael Spindler explains, "Willy counters Ben's competitive individualism with a naïve faith in the power of personal attractiveness as the new Way to Wealth in the highly personalized consumer economy … As he becomes increasingly conscious of the failure of that credo, the image of Ben haunts him with the possibility of what he might have been" (Siebold ed. *Salesman* 62).

Another father-figure, his first employer, Frank Wagner, represents to Willy the old values of business when an employer came to an employee to ask about the naming of his new baby and when verbal promises were made across a desk that would be honored even though they were not written down. Again, we have only Willy's word that these things actually happened, but the point is not whether they happened but that Willy is convinced that they *did* happen. However unrealistic this version of the business world ever was, it is certainly not the world in which Willy now operates. That world is represented by Howard Wagner for whom "business is business" and the only thing that matters is the bottom line. In Howard's world, there is no room for sentiment. He tells Willy, "everybody's gotta pull his own weight," and when Willy's sales drop below a certain level Howard has no hesitation in taking him off salary and putting him on straight commission. Similarly, when Willy fails to keep the appointment in Portland with Brown and Morrison (only the latest of several such failures), Howard uses it as a justification for firing him, *apparently* without giving a second thought to his long service with the firm or to the financial hardship his action will cause. (I have pointed out earlier that Howard is not so ruthless as he sees himself as being.)

Against this reality, Willy has (from the very earliest days of his selling career) constructed a lie in which he is a successful salesman, a valued member of the firm, a loving husband, and an inspirational father: the "illusionist ... has created an image of himself which fails to correspond with Willy Loman as he is ... it's the discrepancy [between the two] that matters ... the discrepancy is so great that it finally slays him" (Garland, Weales ed. 200). Evidently, Willy is *not* Everyman in the sense that he is not presented as representative of salesmen (or more generally of those seeking success in the world of business) in mid-twentieth century America. A. Howard Fuller does, however, define the sense in which he *is* an Everyman figure when he writes, "Willy does represent any man whose illusions have made him incapable of dealing realistically with the problems of everyday life" (Weales ed. 243).

Willy's greatest single disappointment in life is the failure of his talented son, Biff, to make any impression in the world of business, and Biff's subsequent years drifting from low-paid job to another in the West. Willy desperately tries to understand why his relationship with Biff collapsed and why his son failed so completely in business when he had such promise in high school. Willy's consciousness effectively blocks out (represses) his affair with The Woman and Biff's discovery of his infidelity to Linda, so that he lives in a state of denial. Only when that terrible memory reemerges from his subconscious does he begin to understand Biff's failure. Unfortunately, Willy does *not* see that Biff's rejection of him and of everything he stands for is not an act of personal "spite" against his father for betraying his mother. Biff's rejection of the world of selling goes much deeper.

Oedipus blinds himself because he realizes that he has made fatal errors of judgment (i.e., he has not used his eyes when he had them); Othello commits suicide because he realizes that he has been deceived by Iago, and by his own passionate nature, to kill his innocent wife; Macbeth perseveres in a single combat that he knows he must lose because he recognizes that the Witches have exploited his ambition to made foul appear to be fair; and so on. In contrast, Willy approaches the moment self-knowledge typical of the tragic hero, but then backs way from it. As Eric Motram explains, "Loman has been unable to learn that business ethics, the morality of his work community, oppose the traditions he assumed were still in action: the personal ethic of honor, the patriarchal nature of a basically benevolent society and family, and neighborhood relations" (Bloom ed. *Guides* 78). Biff tells his father, "I am not a leader of men, Willy, and neither are you. You were never anything but a hardworking drummer who landed in the ash can like all the rest of them!" Deaf to the truth, Willy's dreams never change, never adapt to developing realities; he dies with *all* of his illusions intact acknowledging neither the real nature of the sales business nor the limitations of his own character.

Why does Willy go to his death for a lie? Why does he go to his death for a lump sum insurance payment that no one (certainly not Biff or Linda) wants? Partly it is that he has invested too much in the image of himself as a success – he measures himself against his own vision of his father and brother and cannot allow himself to be, by comparison, a failure. He tells Ben, "A man can't go out the way he came in ... a man has got to add up to something" – the insurance money will be Willy's legacy, his vindication. In his own mind, he equates his suicide with his father's adventurous pursuit of gold in Alaska and his brother's adventurous pursuit of diamonds in Africa.

The other reason is that Willy has become fixated in believing that the explanation for Biff's failure is his son's spite against him for the discovery of the Boston affair. When Biff cries and begs him to "take that phony dream and burn it before something happens," Willy *sees* the tears, but he does not *hear* the words. Thus, he is able to conclude that the personal spite that has been holding Biff back all these years has vanished because Biff has forgiven him for the Boston incident, and that therefore there is nothing to hold Biff back in the future. He "*cries out his promise*: That boy – that boy is going to be magnificent!" Unfortunately for Willy, he has nothing with which to repay Biff's gift of love other than the gift of the insurance money. This is proof positive that Willy has understood nothing that Biff has tried to tell him. Leonard Moss explains it clearly:

> With his suicide Willy intended to refute the indications that he had failed in his profession, in his family life, and, most important, in his self-estimation. But his insurance money could not possibly efface those indications because Biff has rejected a monetary standard of success – the "something" Willy decides to "add up to." (35)

Critics have made much of the name of this character, frequently using it to label Willy an Everyman figure – despite Miller's own denial that he intended such symbolism when he chose the name. In his autobiographical *Timebends*, Miller tells the story of the origin of his character's name in *The Testament of Dr. Mabuse*, a 1933 German crime movie directed by Fritz Lang, in which there is a character called Inspector Karl Lohmann. Miller comments, "In later years I found it discouraging to observe the confidence with which some commentators of *Death of a Salesman* smirked at the heavy-handed symbolism of 'Low-man.' What the name really meant to me was a terror-stricken man calling into the void for help that will never come." Despite Miller's objections, Willy's surname *does* identify him as literally a *"low man"* – a reality that Willy consistently rejects. There are hundreds of thousands of salesmen in American, and there is nothing exceptional about Willy's performance in that capacity – he scrapes by from pay-check to pay-check, just most of them do. As Biff desperately attempts to tell him, "Pop! I'm a dime a dozen, and so are you!" Recognition of this simple fact would save Willy's life, but he stubbornly resists that truth, convinced (by an act of *willpower*) that he is somehow better than the others and that he is immune from the impersonal rules of business. As Learner and Learner write, "Willy remains blind, even to his death, to the reality that Biff does not want to bear Willy's burden of empty words of success. Willy cannot recognize his son's failures in business, just as he cannot recognize his own" (12). Matthew Roudané explains that Willy's "real condition" (one might rephrase this as 'the real tragedy of Willy's condition') "lies in his insecurity in the universe, his profound sense of being unfulfilled … when he screams, 'I am not a dime a dozen! I am Willy Loman, and you are Biff Loman', is he not laying claim, not only to his dignity and individual worth but also to every person's worthiness?" (Bigsby ed. 82). In this sense, Willy *is* a universal figure.

Linda Loman

> The important question about Linda … is whether she is Willy's constant mainstay ("the perfect wife" to use T. C. Worsley's words) or whether, as Dillingham says, she is a contributing force in his fatal commitment to the wrong dream. (Weales ed. xviii-xix)

The SparkNotes editors describe Linda as "probably the most enigmatic and complex character in *Death of a Salesman*" while Edward Murray comments, "Linda is more [of a] flat [character] than would seem either desirable or necessary" (Siebold ed. *Miller* 115). Both comments seem to be true: Linda is a mass of contradictions, which perhaps explains why she is the character in the play that elicits the most diverse interpretations among critics. However, it is an open question whether, in Linda, Miller can be regarded as having written an artistically satisfying character at all.

If there is one thing that is indisputable, it is that Linda uncritically loves and is unconditionally devoted to her husband: for most of the play, she acts like the stereotypical submissive wife-as-homemaker of the 1940s. She tells Biff, "He's the dearest man in the world to me, and I won't have anyone making him feel blue," though what the audience sees scarcely supports such an assertion. Linda will protect her husband at any cost, and when she has to choose, Linda has no hesitation in choosing Willy over her two sons. In the end, however, she fails to protect Willy from his own pursuit of what he considers to be success. Some critics go so far as to blame her for enabling his suicide. Brian Parker does not mince words writing, "Surely it is both stupid and immoral to encourage the man you love in self-deceit and lies" (Bloom ed. *Interpretations* 36).

In many ways, Linda is a realist. It is she who manages the money and pays the bills, which is no easy task since the size of the bills always seems to be greater than the sum of money available. She measures success much more modestly than her husband. For Linda, owning a house after having paid off a twenty-five year mortgage is a real "accomplishment." Unlike Willy, who wants Biff to inherit the house and live there with his own family, Linda knows that children grow up and move out. For her, the house has "served its purpose" in providing a place to bring up the children; she understands that "life is a casting off" and is not frightened by that as is Willy, who desperately wants to leave his children a legacy when he dies because that will establish a continuity which will in turn validate his belief system and himself. Linda has no such ideals.

Neither does Linda share her husband's conviction that "the man who makes an appearance in the business world, the man who creates personal interest, is the man who gets ahead." For one thing, getting ahead of the other guy is not important to Linda; she only wants a husband and sons who earn enough to afford the necessities of a comfortable middle class life. She has no higher aspirations. For another thing, unlike Willy, Linda places much more emphasis on basic ethics and hard work as the key to success in life. It is she who expresses concern over Biff's poor math performance, his growing aggression (particularly toward the girls), and his propensity for stealing – all things that Willy either overlooks, condones or actively encourages.

Although Linda is practical and resourceful, she faces challenges which are beyond her power to deal with. From the time her children were teens (and presumably earlier), Linda has seen through her husband's lies about his success, but she has never had the courage to call him out and confront him with the truth of his own mediocrity. A realist herself, she does everything she can to protect Willy from reality. The apparent contradiction is explained by Linda's own need to achieve financial security. She knows that her husband is not a top salesman, but in pursuit of her own dream of owning their house and becoming, as she says in "Requiem," "free and clear," she feeds his illusion because Willy's is the only source of income in the house and, with her encouragement, he can keep bringing in just enough for the family to get by. There is nothing cynical or selfish about Linda's motivation, but the fact remains that she does prevent Willy from learning the truth about who he actually is until it is too late for him to make that kind of adjustment that (it appears) Biff is going to make at the end of the play.

The paradox of Linda's character is that, while she can be firm and brutally honest with her sons, with her husband she is incapable of such honesty. Now, when he is sixty-three, she knows that Willy is heading for a nervous breakdown, that he is contemplating suicide and may already have attempted suicide by crashing his car. However, since she has no real understanding of what drives Willy, she cannot empathize with him. She can do no more than try to ameliorate the pressure on Willy in the hope of taking away his motive for suicide. This is why she will do anything to bolster his sense of hope, even though she knows that the hope engendered is based upon an illusion and that (like the 'high' of a drug) it will only be temporary. She accepts his bullying and insensitivity because she knows how fragile Willy's ego is; she hides from Willy her knowledge that he is working on commission and borrowing money from Charley because she knows that to reveal it would humiliate Willy; she does not confront him with the rubber piping because she knows that it would shame him.

In many ways, Linda's avoidance strategies only make Willy's delusions worse; indeed, it can certainly be argued that Linda's coping strategies make her complicit in his death. However, she does not know what else to do. Harold Bloom writes, "Using the only resources they can summon, Willy and Linda create a kind of false consciousness about the turmoil at the center of their lives" (*Guides* 27).

The one area in which Linda does take action is trying to mend Willy's broken relationship with his two sons, apparently believing that if his sons can "become successful then Willy's fragile psyche will heal itself" (ThoughtCo.). At first, when the boys are newly arrived home, she attempts to recreate the atmosphere in the house when Biff and Happy were teens. When this fails because of arguments between Willy and Biff, she tries (and inevitably fails) to get to the bottom of Biff's antagonism towards his father. Her failure has one of two explanations: either she genuinely does not *know* about Willy's affair(s) on the road because Willy and Biff conspire to keep her ignorant of the Boston incident; or, as with everything else, Linda *is* aware that her lonely husband had at least one affair but (again as with every other truth she knows about Willy) she chooses not openly to acknowledge it. Either way, the wound cannot be healed unless it is brought out into the open, and Linda is incapable of doing that.

Once matters reach a crisis after Biff and Happy have walked out on Willy at Frank's Chop House, she does confront them with the shortcomings of their lives and with the way in which they are hurting their father, "Get out of here, both of you, and don't come back! I don't want you tormenting him any more." Linda's motivation here is to protect Willy from the hurtful influence of his sons rather than to deal with the fundamental causes of Happy's womanizing, Biff's drifting and Willy's mental breakdown. As Domina points out, "She fails to consider the possibility that Biff's instability and the immaturity of both Biff and Happy have been affected by Willy's model" (Learner and Learner ed. 45). Linda is doing no more than papering over the cracks. Like Willy, she is on stage when Biff tries to explain the understanding he has come to about his father's "phony dream" and the damage it has done to every member of the family, but she appears to understand what Biff is saying no more than does Willy. She simply tries to get Willy to come to bed, confident that, having got his sons out of Willy's life, "It's all settled now." She has no idea that Happy, Biff, Willy and herself each have completely different ideas about how the situation can be settled.

Linda's failure to understand is confirmed in the "Requiem" where she asks, "Why didn't anybody come?" Knowing what she did about Willy's failed career in sales; knowing that those contacts he once did have are now retired or dead; knowing that Howard fired him, Linda *still* expected crowds of people to attend the funeral? (Compare Willy's expectation, "Ben, that funeral will be massive! They'll come from Maine, Massachusetts, Vermont, New Hampshire! ... – that boy will be thunder-struck ... he'll see it with his eyes once and for all.") Of course, no one comes – even Howard does not come. Linda also admits that she "can't understand" why Willy killed himself because financially they were "free and clear." She did not share his dream of success and would have been satisfied on "a little salary," but how could she not have understood it? Even Charley understands Willy better than Linda.

ThoughtCo. makes the argument that *Death of a Salesman* is also Linda's tragedy:

> Her life, however, is dreary because she always hopes that things will work out for the better – yet those hopes never blossom. They always wither.
>
> Her one major decision takes place before the action of the play. She chooses to marry and emotionally support Willy Loman, a man who wanted to be great but defined greatness as being "well-liked" by others. Because of Linda's choice, the rest of her life will be filled with disappointment.

This is a perfectly reasonable interpretation (and one that some other critics have also proposed). However, Linda remains a character whose situation is *potentially* tragic rather than a fully developed tragic character – there simply is not the depth of psychological insight in Miller's characterization of Linda who remains a paradox: a complex but flat character.

Biff Loman

Biff is very like his father except that in Biff the family's "adventurous ... streak of self-reliance" seems to be much stronger. Nevertheless, he is similarly divided between his love of manual work in the open air and his feeling that he *ought* to achieve something tangible with his life, something he can pass on to his children, which he can only win in the business world. He tells Happy, "There's nothing more inspiring or – beautiful than the sight of a mare and a new colt," but notice the hesitation before the word "beautiful" as though he is ashamed to use it. We are not surprised when he continues, "whenever spring comes to where I am, I suddenly get to feeling, my God, I'm not gettin' anywhere ... I'm a boy. I'm not married, I'm not in business, I just - I'm like a boy." Biff is being pulled apart because the emotional contentment he has found in the West (an American symbol of freedom) is continually undermined by his father's version of the American Dream which defines success and happiness in purely material terms. As a result, Willy sees his favorite son as an under-achiever: he blames Biff's failure to make good in the business world on mere spite (stemming from the Boston incident) because the alternative would be to acknowledge the fundamental flaws in his own vision and values. The reality that Willy never acknowledges but that Biff finally comes to understand is that Biff is *constitutionally incapable* of playing the role in business that Willy has determined that he should play. Bigsby points out that while Willy feels guilt over the Boston incident (because he knows that it was the immediate cause of Biff's decision to 'drop out), "Biff equally feels guilty because he recognizes a responsibility which he cannot fulfill. The responsibility to redeem Willy's empty life" (Siebold ed. *Miller* 126). Biff cannot find peace in the West because he has been brought up to view life as "competition, a restless pursuit of success, a desire to register a material achievement which [he] can only conceive in financial terms" (Ibid 127).

The turning point in Biff's life comes just before the end of his senior year in high school when he discovers that his father has a mistress. This immediately strips Biff of his faith in Willy both as a person and as a role model. Suddenly, Biff realizes that Willy's façade of success is false and that his dream is not worth pursuing. As Bigsby explains, from this point on, "Biff ... feels guilty because he recognizes a responsibility which he cannot fulfil, the responsibility to redeem Willy's empty life" (Bloom ed. *Interpretations* 118). He is estranged from his father; he feels that he must seek the truth about himself, but he is poorly prepared for such a quest. In fact, unconsciously Biff uses his anger at his father as an excuse for not looking within himself to discover the true reasons for his failure.

Having basically refused to graduate high school, and thus to lose the three university scholarships, the unqualified Biff takes an entry-level clerking job in Bill Oliver's firm, but loses that job when, thwarted in his unrealistic expectation of quick promotion, he takes to petty theft. This is the pattern of Biff's life until he finally has the courage to move out of the city and take jobs herding cattle in Nebraska, the Dakotas, Arizona, and Texas. Although he is contented living this sort of life, Biff still cannot acknowledge that his failure in the business-world is *not* a personal failure but a basic flaw in the vision and values that Willy taught him. That is why, when spring comes around, he finds himself drawn back to New York, and, as he tells Happy, "every time I come back here I know that all I have done is to waste my life" – the truth, of course, is the very reverse of that. The Biff we meet at the start of the play is a man still trapped, against his deepest inclinations, in Willy's dream of success in the business world. He steals items which symbolize the business executive he will never be: a suit in Kansas City and a pen in New York.

After his epiphany in Bill Oliver's office, Biff understands that the fundamental problem is his father's "phony dream." Having understood what he needs to do with his own life in order to reclaim his true identity, Biff tries to break through the lies and self-deception that have ruined the lives of every member of the Loman family. He tells Willy, "Today I realized something about myself ... and I – I think I'm just not smart enough to make any sense out of it for you." Biff is right: he gives his father the gift of his love (wiping out the Boston hotel incident) and in return, as Miller explained to Chinese actor playing the part, what he really wants is "to resolve this conflict ... to get his [father's] blessing, to be able to cast off his heavy hand and free [himself]" (Griffin 47). What he gets is $20,000. Biff should not blame himself for his failure: the truth is that Happy, Linda and Willy have too much invested in their illusions to accept harsh reality at this point in their lives.

Reflecting on the play one year after its premier, Miller admitted to "certain disappointments, one above all. I am sorry that the self-realization of the older son, Biff, is not a weightier counterbalance to Willy's disaster in the audience mind" (Weales ed. 150). There is, however, an argument that, whatever Miller intended, Biff is the true protagonist of the play. Certainly Biff is the one character with whom the audience relates. Weales explains this view (which he does not share) pointing out that because "plays customarily deal with some kind of discovery and since Willy's recognition of Biff's love does not alter his basic self-delusion about success, the audience's attention, sympathy, concern turn to Biff..." (xvii). Another way of saying the same thing is that Biff is the only *round* character in the play; all of the other characters are *flat*. Only Biff develops (or at least has the potential for development); only Biff has the capacity to learn. Every other character is the same person at the end of the play as he/she was at the beginning[1].

[1."We may divide characters into flat and round. Flat characters were called "humours" in the seventeenth century, and are sometimes called types, and sometimes caricatures. In their purest form, they are constructed round a single idea or quality ... The test of a round character is whether it is capable of surprising in a convincing way. If it never surprises, it is flat" (E. M. Forster *Aspects of the Novel* 1927).]

Happy Loman

Just like his father, Happy suffers from being the overlooked second son, and the remarkable thing is that Willy (who is uniquely placed to ensure that Happy does not suffer as he did from the absence of paternal support) does not realize this basic similarity. Happy is always trying to get his father's attention away from Biff and gain some token of Willy's approval, and we can see this in the way he has gone into selling. The divided psyche that we have identified in Willy and Biff, appears to be much less obvious in Happy who is a less conflicted version of his father. The SparkNotes editors point out that "Happy shares none of the poetry that erupts from Biff and that is buried in Willy." Oscar Brockett explains why:

> Happy has inherited the worst of Will's traits without the saving possibility of love. He is entirely selfish and unfeeling; lying and cheating are integral parts of his nature. He is a materialist and sensualist beyond redemption, but devoid of Ben's vision and strength. (Siebold ed. *Miller* 100)

Of course, Happy knows nothing about his father having a mistress and so has never been forced to see through Willy's façade to the emptiness that it so imperfectly covers. Thus, Happy has never questioned either his father's belief in success or his advice about the personal qualities that will bring that success. As Harold Clurman states, "[Happy] believes only that his father is an incompetent ... but he does not reject his father's dream" (Weales ed. 214).

Nevertheless, at the start of the play, Happy recognizes that his apartment, his car and his women do not add up to a satisfying life. He feels himself to be physically superior to all of the men above him who stand in his way, and compensates by seducing their women – although even this is not an ultimately satisfying form of revenge. Happy is not climbing the corporate ladder as quickly as Willy led him to believe that he would, since, as he tells Biff, the reality is that "All I can do is wait for the merchandise manager to die." Like Willy, Happy compensates by exaggerating his position in order to create an illusion of success, claiming to be the assistant buyer when he is just an assistant to the assistant – just as Willy inflates his sales numbers and Biff remembers being a salesman for Bill Oliver when he was merely a clerk. Happy's claim that manufacturer's offer him hundred dollar bribes to steer business their way also sounds like an inflated boast given his lowly position in the firm. More fundamentally, however, Happy has seen that even financial success in the business world does not bring happiness. He tells Biff about his friend, the merchandise manager, who earns enough to build "a terrific estate on Long Island" but then sells it because he cannot enjoy it once it is finished. Happy defines his problem, "I don't know what the hell I'm workin' for."

Happy is consistently overlooked by his father in favor of his more charismatic elder brother, and Linda (somewhat inexplicably) repeatedly shows the same preference. If both are disappointed by Biff's failure, it seems that they half-expected Happy to fail. Nothing that he does seems to gain him his patents' approval. No one disputes his assertion that he has just paid for Linda and Willy to take a vacation in Florida (no small financial sacrifice given his modest salary), but he gets no credit for it. As Bernard Dukore argues, "The neglected son has his revenge ... on his father and brother through philandering. By refusing to marry, he rejects his father's value system; to prove he is more of a man than his brother, an athletic hero, he excels in the sexual arena" (Siebold ed. *Salesman* 123). He gets his ultimate revenge when, in the restaurant he tells Miss Forsythe that Willy is "not my father. He's just a guy."

Happy's dilemma is arguably worse than Biff's because Happy lacks any alternative: he lacks Biff's idealism. Never having been disillusioned about his father's dream as Biff was by the Boston incident, and having no affinity with the outdoors and manual work, Happy has nowhere else to go. Kay Stanton comments that "Happy uses women as Ben used the jungle and timberlands, and he carves out a territory for himself as Ben had ... Happy sought the self-confidence of the older brother Biff and found sexual confidence, and it is now where he has superiority over his brother" (Bloom ed. *Loman* 133). His highest aspiration is to marry a woman like his mother and settle down to the sort of idyllic family life that he wrongly imagines his parents have had, but he will never do that either. Proof positive that Happy has learned nothing from the events of the play is his empty promise to "show ... everyone else that Willy Loman did not die in vain. He had a good dream. It's the only dream you can have – to come out number-one man. He fought it out here, and this is where I'm gonna win it for him." Notice that Happy's speech here is merely a collection of clichés. The whole thrust of the play has been to show that Willy's dream is "phony" and that there are alternatives to it which are real.

Ben Loman

We can be pretty certain that Ben Loman actually existed, that he made his fortune in Africa and followed-up with investments in Alaska, that he visited the Loman house in Brooklyn on two occasions, and that he has died recently. We know these things because they are discussed in the real-time scenes of the play. Beyond this, however, it is very difficult to determine the truth about Ben since so much depends upon Willy's imagination. Brian Parker writes that "Ben seems less 'real' that the others [i.e., other characters] because he is not so much a person as the embodiment of Will's desire for escape and success" (Bloom ed. *Interpretations* 29). Onto the character of Ben, Willy projects those qualities of self-assurance, ruthlessness, lack of scruples and simple good luck that he admires but knows himself to lack.

Willy idolizes Ben who is both his role model and his alter ego. Like their father, Ben is a self-sufficient, rugged, outdoor adventurer. Willy ignores the fact that Ben makes his fortune by finding diamonds in the African jungle; that is, that Ben loots the wealth in the raw materials of a colonial country and thus represents the last of the robber barons who, in the nineteenth century, ruthlessly exploited native populations to amass great fortunes. In terms of the American Dream, Ben embodies the old-fashioned idea that a man can set out alone into the wilderness and come back wealthy. The days of such men are over: the American frontier had been declared closed following the U.S. Census of 1890, and the tide of colonialism began to ebb following World War I. Despite all of this, Willy sees his elder brother as a symbol that his dreams of making it big in the business world are realistic. Willy expresses his belief that the new jungle is the business world when he tells Ben, "It's who you know and the smile on your face! It's contacts, Ben, contacts! The whole wealth of Alaska passes over the lunch table at the Commodore Hotel, and that's the wonder, the wonder of this country, that a man can end with diamonds here on the basis of being liked!" What he does not realize is that the men sitting around that table were born rich.

Ben proves to be an unhelpful mentor to Willy. We are never told just *how* he made his fortune in Africa, probably because Willy does not know. It seems to be a case of dumb luck and a faulty sense of geography that put him in the right place at the right time together with a ruthless streak. He does tell Willy, "The jungle is dark but full of diamonds." The darkness here suggests moral darkness: Ben probably got his diamonds illegally. Certainly, Ben is a man who would never let morality get in the way of profit. When Ben spars with Biff, he wins because he cheats. Ben tells Biff that the only way to win is, "Never [to] fight fair with a stranger." However, Willy does not have that kind of ruthlessness in him. One of Willy's repeated regrets is that he did not go to Alaska when Ben offered him a job there, but it would have been completely out of character for Willy to have done so. Ben is a risk-taker; Willy is not.

By the end of the play when Willy discusses with Ben the idea of committing suicide so that Biff will have the insurance money (a legacy that will both vindicate Willy's life and give Biff the capital he needs to start his own business), Ben has become a cipher for Willy's own ideas, as when he tells Willy, "twenty thousand – that is something one can feel in the hand, it is there." Willy seems to put these words into Ben's mouth in order to persuade himself that he will finally have done something comparable to his elder brother coming out of the jungle with diamonds.

Frank and Howard Wagner

Howard inherited the company from its founder his father, Frank Wagner. It is entirely possible that Willy romanticizes his close relationship with Old Man Wagner. For example, Willy did *not* name Howard; his boss merely asked him what he "thought of the name Howard" – which is very different. Nor does it seem likely that Frank ever made promises to Willy about his future with the firm because Willy was such an exceptional sales representative. Nevertheless, Willy still thinks of Frank as "a masterful man" and "a prince." In contrast, the thirty-six-year-old Howard represents for Willy the new, impersonal face of business for whom concepts such as loyalty, respect, friendship no longer have value. A very rich man himself, he simply cannot grasp, and certainly cannot empathize with, Willy's financial crisis.

For Howard, "business is business" means that anyone who does not pull his weight is out. Thus, he is quite prepared to take Willy off salary and to lie about not being able to find a slot for him in the New York office. Finally, he uses Willy's latest failure as an excuse to fire him, but he is businessman enough to make sure to remind Willy to "stop by and drop off the samples" some time "this week." Ironically, he is the somewhat less ruthless twentieth century equivalent of Ben Loman.

Charley

Charley is Willy's long-term neighbor and, at the time of the play's action, his only remaining friend. He shows his friendship by loaning Willy $50 a week after Willy has been taken off salary and by repeatedly offering him a job. (This is a clear contrast with Howard, who certainly *could* find Willy a New York job if he wanted to.) Charley knows Willy well and understand what drives him better than any of the other characters – even better that Linda. This is because Charley has no illusions.

The two men are very different. Charley is a pragmatist who values education, hard-work and honesty, while Willy is an idealist (or dreamer if you prefer) who believes that success depends upon appearance, personality and a willingness to disregard the rules. Charley has a strict view of morality. When Willy, who is trying to impress Ben, sends the boys to the construction site to steal sand, Charley tells him, "Listen, if they steal any more from that building, the watchman'll put the cops on them!" Charley turns out to be right about the values Willy is inculcating because Biff will later admit to having spent time in jail for three months because he "stole a suit in Kansas City."

Charley is a modest man while Willy is boastful. Brian Parker concludes, "For all his sympathetic qualities … Charlie's position is shown to be a compromise: he has succeeded in fitting his character into the existing system, meeting business on its own cold terms" (Bloom ed. *Interpretations* 34). Charley is less passionate, less imaginative and less idealistic than is Willy; but, unlike Willy, Charley knows who he is and is content with what he is.

Willy boasts to his two adolescent boys that "Someday I'll have my own business ... Bigger than Uncle Charley! Because Charley is not liked. He's liked, but he's not – well liked." Of course, Willy never achieves his aim while, Charley does own a business which presumably thrives because it offers a service or product that people want at a reasonable price and not because its owner is personally charismatic. Charley does not appear to put pressure on his son Bernard about his future, while Willy instills in Biff and Happy the idea that they must succeed in business. Willy claims that Charley "never told [Bernard] what to do ... never took any interest in him." Despite Charley's self-deprecating reply, "My salvation is that I never took any interest in anything," Willy is only half right. It is true that Charley did not dictate the career that Bernard should follow, but he did set him an example of success, encouraged him to value education, and exemplified the values that would enable Bernard to succeed at whatever *he chose* to do.

Willy's awareness that Charley has succeeded where he has failed causes him to feel puzzlement, pain and resentment. Knowing this, Charley always has to be very careful not to antagonize Willy when he offers him help or simply companionship. Charley is normally very calm, but there are limits. Occasionally, Willy's desperate need to humiliate Charley (e.g., by telling him he does not know about vitamins, by mocking his lack of handyman skills, by accusing him of cheating at cards, etc.) produces an angry reaction in this modest, long-suffering man, as when he tells Willy a harsh truth, "You been jealous of me all your life, you damned fool!" At other times, however, Charley is someone to whom Willy can open up and be completely honest about his financial situation and his sense of having failed, and this is because Charley is not judgmental.

It is often said that the touching eulogy that Charley delivers in the Requiem is out of character. Certain aspects of Charley's behavior at the grave-side are entirely consistent with what we have seen before: his care and compassion for Linda; his skepticism about Happy's claim, "There was no necessity for it. We would've helped him"; and his understanding of human dignity when he says, "No man only needs a little salary." The point at issue is Charley's long speech about the nature of being a salesman. The essential point he makes is that a salesman is alienated (in the Marxist sense) from both production and consumption. Having no connection to the product he sells, a salesman must necessarily be selling himself with "a smile and a shoeshine," and when buyers stop being impressed because there are other salesmen with wider smiles and shinier shoes, the salesman knows he is finished. A craftsman can take pride in his work, a lawyer in his verdicts and a doctor in his cures, but

"A salesman got to dream ... It comes with the territory." That seems to be true, and it seems to be what Charley has known all along and to be why he has been so supportive of Willy. However, Charley's repeated conclusion, "Nobody dast blame this man" seems to conflate having a dream of success to keep oneself motivated with Willy's very personal "phony dream" – a dream that negatively impacts the lives of his wife and sons. Willy is *not* a typical salesman, and Charley *ought* to know that. As Joseph Hynes puts it, Charley's speech "speaks of the salesman rather than of the particular salesman in question. Furthermore, it denies the character of Charley, who cannot possibly believe what he is saying, since his part is that of the clear-eyed realist" (Weales ed. 283).

Bernard

It is worth repeating that the scenes from the past in the play are not objective representations of what actually happened; they are recreations of past evens through the distorting lens of Willy's disintegrating mind. No single character illustrates this better than Bernard since the adolescent and the adult characters are so very different. Of course, in fifteen years people can change a lot, but I think that the play's real point is that Bernard was never the "pest ... anemic ... worm" that Willy re-imagines. Bernard tells Willy that when Biff got back from Boston the two "had a fist fight. It lasted at least half an hour." The Bernard whom Willy remembers would not have stood up to Biff for five minutes.

Like his father, Bernard is a pragmatist. After Biff shows that he has printed 'University of Virginia' on his shoes, Bernard comments sensibly, "Just because he printed University of Virginia on his sneakers doesn't mean they've got to graduate him, Uncle Willy!" Bernard never mistakes bluster for solid achievement. Just as Charley helps Willy, so Bernard helps Biff by trying to get him to take his studies seriously, but he draws the line at passing him the answers in the graduation examination because "That's a state exam! They're liable to arrest me!" There is no reason to doubt that he looked up to Biff in school, but Willy's memories probably exaggerate the degree to which he did so. In the hero-worshiping Young Bernard, Willy creates an example of the sort of impact on people that he expected Biff to have throughout his life.

When he meets Bernard in Charley's office, Willy is "*surprised ... almost shocked*" to see him carrying tennis rackets and to learn that he is a man with friends who "have their own tennis court." Bernard is married with two children while Willy's boys remain unmarried. Bernard, like his father, is modest; he does not tell Willy (who is boasting to him about Biff, "doing very big things in the West" and how, "Bill Oliver – very big sporting-goods man – ... wants Biff very badly") that he is about to argue a case before the Supreme Court, because, as Charley explains, "He don't have to [mention it] – he's gonna do it." Bernard shows what Happy and Biff might have become had not Willy's "phony dream" destroyed their lives.

Structure

> [N]othing in life comes 'next ... everything exists together, and at the same time within us' ... there is no past to be 'brought forward' in a human being ... he is his past at every moment ... I wanted to create a form which, in itself as a form, would literally be the process of Willy Loman's way of mind. (Miller "Introduction to Collected Plays," Weales ed.156)

The play has around forty scenes. There are no formal divisions; one scene flows into the next so fluidly that it is sometimes impossible to say precisely where one ends and the next begins. The stage set contains a number of rooms in the house and other spaces that, with a few props and a lighting change, can be used immediately. As a result, the audience does not have to wait for scene changes, but instead moves instantaneously from scene to scene, from objective to subjective reality. Such fluid movement, without time delays or dialogue transitions, produces a continuous sequence of events which portray what is happening in real time and what is happening in Willy Loman's mind.

The original stage designer, Jo Mielzinger, reports that Miller himself had no idea how his play would be staged beyond the warning that, "'The scenic solution to this production will have to be an imaginative and simple one'" ("Designing a Play: *Death of a Salesman*," Weales ed. 187). The essential challenge of the designer is that "Actors playing exactly a contemporaneous scene suddenly went back fifteen years in exactly the same setting – the Salesman's house..." (Ibid. 188). Getting the actors playing Biff and Happy from their beds in an upper story of the house to the stage floor ready to enter as their adolescent selves in Act One proved to be particularly difficult. This raises the interesting question of why no productions actually use younger actors to play the parts of Biff, Happy and Bernard. The answer is that the scenes from the past which are interspersed with the real time contemporaneous action are not flashbacks; that is, they are not objective recreations of the past. These scenes are happening in the 'now' of the play, but they are happening inside Willy Loman's head. They are not objective; on the contrary, they are totally subjective imaginings which usually begin by presenting the past as Willy desperately needs to believe that it was (i.e., the idyllic past) but quickly degenerate into warnings of the disasters to come because the part of Willy's mind that he cannot control (i.e., his subconscious) feeds into these scenes his knowledge of later events. As the play progresses, Willy is less and less able to distinguish between his memories of the past and the realities of the present.

Themes

Willy Loman has a belief system which justifies his dual roles as a salesman for the Wagner Company and as the patriarch of the Loman family. Of his role in the business world, he has convinced himself that:
- selling is a noble calling that depends upon honor and respect between people;
- he is a successful salesman because his personality makes him well-liked by buyers;
- he opened up the New England market and is crucial to the firm's continued success there;
- he has a record of outstanding sales over three decades that entitle him to expect special treatment by the boss.

Of his role as patriarch, he has convinced himself that:
- he is a loving husband and devoted father whose wife and sons idolize him;
- he is teaching his boys the skills and values that will ensure their success in business;
- his boys will achieve a level of success beyond that he himself achieved, but in doing so will validate his own dreams.

As Hoeveler comments, "All these conceptions are, of course, delusions but, unfortunately, they are believed to some degree by all the family members" (Bloom ed. *Interpretations* 78). As a result, their reality becomes what Willy wants (and increasingly needs) it to be and objectivity is impossible.

The American Dream

> [T]here are two versions of the American dream. The historical American dream is the promise of a land of freedom with opportunity and equality for all. This dream needs no challenge, only fulfillment. But since the Civil War, and particularly since 1900, the American dream has become distorted to the dream of business success. The original premise ... was that enterprise, courage and hard work were the keys to success. Since the end of the First World War this too has changed. Instead of the ideals of hard work and courage, we have salesmanship ... The goal of salesmanship is to make a deal, to earn a profit – the accumulation of profit being an unquestioned end in itself. (Clurman "The Success Dream on the American Stage," Weales ed. 212-213).

Entire books have been written on the American dream, so it is unlikely that a simple definition will meet with general acceptance. Nevertheless, it is important to note that the dream has changed over time. In the nineteenth century, success was defined as making enough through one's own efforts to live well, but in the twentieth century, it became defined as making more through one's own efforts than anyone else. Over the same period, the dream changed its locale from the untamed frontier to the concrete jungle. Willy Loman, born in the nineteenth century, was raised to follow a dream that was in the process of changing beyond recognition. William Heyen clearly describes the consequences, "The American Dream is rural, not urban, and the perfect world is out there somewhere, and when we can't find it out there ahead if us, we go back to the elm-shaded past" (Bloom ed. *Interpretations* 54).

Psychological Defense Mechanisms

Sigmund Freud (1856-1939), the founder of psychoanalysis, was the first to describe a variety of defenses that are unconsciously used by the fragile ego to protect itself from anxiety generated by unacceptable thoughts or feelings and threatening realities. Repression is a mechanism employed to prevent disturbing thoughts from becoming conscious. Willy is the only member of the Loman family to practice repression: he has repressed all knowledge of his encounter with Biff in Boston, unlike Biff who remembers it only too well. The incident destroyed the self that Biff had allowed his father to construct, and Willy's ego knows that the reemergence of the repressed memory will destroy his own ego. Nevertheless, as Freud pointed out, repression is merely a temporary and an unreliable defense. As the action of the play progresses, the truth comes closer and closer to forcing itself upon Will's consciousness and shattering his ego.

Psychological defense mechanisms frequently work together to protect the ego, and in addition to repression, Willy also lives in denial. He is incapable of accepting the fact that he has *always* been a mediocre salesman. To do this, he is forced to deny reality: he lies to both Linda and Howard about the sales he has made; he hides the fact that he has been placed on commission and is borrowing $50 a week from Charley to make up his wages; he recreates the past in his imagination in ways that conform to his view of how it should have been. Each of the Lomans is also living in denial and by doing so is perpetuating denial in the others. Perhaps Linda once believed Willy's boasts, but years of trying to balance the family budget have shown her the truth that she has never had the courage to face. Perhaps Biff once believed both in Willy's dream and in his father's capacity to attain success; as an adult he knows the truth but refuses to acknowledge it. Happy has bought into Willy's lies more completely than Biff; as an adult, he knows that his father is not the hot shot salesman he has claimed to be, but he continues to deny the evidence of his own experience that the holy grail of success in business is not worth attaining.

Biff has much greater self-knowledge, particularly after his epiphany in Bill Oliver's office, but even then he is almost persuaded to conceal the truth behind lies about Oliver's interest in his proposal. Even when Biff finally speaks the truth (i.e., neither Willy, nor Happy, nor himself is capable of achieving success and success is not worth attaining) all of the other family members retain what tattered elements of denial they can: Linda will simply let Biff leave without changing anything about the way she supports Willy's illusions; Willy will kill himself to get Biff the start-up capital that, against his clear statement to the contrary, he is convinced that Biff wants and needs; and Happy will seek to prove that, though his father was not able to fulfill achieve it, his dream of coming out on top was valid after all.

The tension of the play rests in the conflict between repression/denial and the inevitable reemergence of memories and present realities which threaten to destroy Willy's defense mechanisms. The crisis of the drama comes when Willy can no longer live his life as though the Boston hotel incident never happened. The sadness of the plays conclusion (at the premier, members of the audience were often reduced to tears) result from Will's failure to free himself from the denial mechanisms that allow him, despite all evidence to the contrary, to continue to believe in his dreams of success.

The Place of Women

The roles played by women in the play has received harsh criticism particularly from feminist critics. I think it would be pointless to argue with Kay Stanton's conclusion that "Careful analysis reveals that the American Dream as presented in *Death of a Salesman* is male-orientated, but it requires unacknowledged dependence upon women as well as women's subjugation and exploitation" (Bloom ed. *Loman* 129). It is men (grandfather Loman and Ben) who stride out alone to make their fortunes in the green frontiers of the world, and it is men (Singleman, Frank, Howard, Bill, Charley and Willy) who struggle, with varying degrees of success, to make their fortunes in the city. The woman's place is to look after the children and keep the home. Grandmother Loman is abandoned by her husband to look after two children and then her seventeen-year-old eldest son leaves her to provide for her remaining three-year-old. To accomplish what she did, grandmother Loman must have been a remarkable woman, but the text tells us virtually nothing more about her. Ben calls her a "[f]ine specimen of a lady" and the "old girl" (a very patronizing oxymoron), but there is no evidence that either he or his father ever saw her again after they walked out. Nor does Willy give any account of his relationship with his mother as a young man deciding on a career. We learn only that she "died a long time ago." Miller just does not seem to be interested.

Linda is similarly a homemaker, a stay-at-home mom who brings up the children and manages the household finances while her husband goes out (leaving her alone for most of the week) to earn the money. When it comes, however, to forming the lives of Biff and Happy, Willy leaves Linda no influence: it is he who instills in them the ambition to succeed in business.

91

Repeatedly, Willy silences his wife because business is a man's world about which women can know nothing. (In passing, we may add that the slight sketch of Howard's wife shows exactly the same tendency.) In so far as they have any role in the business world, women are menials. They are the bosses' secretaries. Jenny, Charley's secretary, is a protective motherly figure who does her best to protect her boss from being upset, and The Woman is a buyer's secretary. In this role, they are the gate-keepers who can show someone through to the boss or keep them in the waiting room. Thus Jenny diverts Willy and Bill Oliver's secretary stalls Biff.

The only other power that women have is their sexuality which they exploit somewhat ruthlessly for their own advantage. The Woman swops access to the boss and sex for stockings (which were, at the time, both highly desirable fashion items and prohibitively expensive). Bill Oliver's secretary gets Biff to ask her on a date (though she exerts her power by turning him down). Miss Forsythe and Letta are so obviously "on call" that critics frequently refer to them as prostitutes – which they are not. What they are is attractive young woman who know the power that their looks give them (and presumably also know that that power will have a limited shelf-life). They are more than prepared to sleep with a man in return for being bought champagne and shown a good time. Happy is entirely hypocritical when he denounces the women that he sleeps with as lacking morals, but (even allowing for a little exaggeration) he does not find it hard to seduce women; he can get sex "any time" he wants it' and he can get his brother "any babe" Biff wants.

Women in the play thus seem reduced to one of two roles: mother or whore. The former (Linda, Mrs. Wagner, and possibly Jenny) are given exaggerated respect by the men and the latter (every other female character) are despised and objectified by men – they are "gorgeous creatures" not people. Stanton concludes, "The double standard is in full force, women are allowed no sexual adventurism: one real or supposed sexual experience and they are 'ruined' forever by male standards" (Bloom ed. *Loman* 134). One might argue, of course, that this is precisely Miller's intention in the play, that *Salesman* is both an accurate depiction of American society as the 1940s came to an end and a denunciation of the subjugation of women by men. The problem is that the text does not support such an interpretation. In this play, at least, Miller appears not to understand women and to be incapable of writing convincing female characters.

Symbols

Major Symbols

The Loman House

The Loman house is established as visual symbol at the very start of the play. It is confined and overlooked by menacing apartment buildings, although a simple lighting change indicates a time when the house stood in a semi-rural spot amongst trees that left it open to the light. Throughout the play, the encroaching buildings are shown to destroy the natural beauty of the original setting of the house. This symbolizes progressive restriction that is contrasted with the vast open spaces of the American West, Alaska, and Africa which represent freedom, independence and opportunity. The house symbolizes Willy, who has worked on it for decades, yet despite his efforts the modern world has closed in on the house and will soon sweep it away in the name of progress. In this way, it represents the futility of Willy's dream of making something permanent through selling.

Music

Different kinds of music are used throughout the play to set the tone of specific scenes and to represent individual characters. The flute music, "*small and fine, telling of grass and trees and the horizon*" that opens and closes the play and recurs at times throughout symbolizes the link that Willy still has, through his father, with the natural world. Grandfather Loman made and sold flutes while traveling around the country: this is his music, the music that Willy tells Ben he remembers hearing as a child. The flute is the sound of an identity and a life that Willy rejected when he decided to become a salesman. In the last few hours of Willy's failed life, it represents nostalgia for a lost world and lost opportunities.

There are, however, different forms of music in the play. There is the intrusive music which accompanies the entrances of Ben, and the "*music of the Boys*" which is contemporary, "*gay and bright.*" The latter is heard at the beginning of Act 2, representing the false optimistic mood and deluded sense of hope that has taken over the family. Intrusive, discordant music introduces Willy recollections of his affair, "*Music is heard as behind a scrim, to the left of the house; The Woman, dimly seen, is dressing.*" At the moment when it becomes inevitable that Willy will relive the incident in the Boston hotel, "*A single trumpet note jars the ear,*" and "*Raw, sensuous music accompanies*" the dialogue between Willy and The Woman, though it ends just before Biff enters and discovers the two together. When Willy offers to fight Charley just before the Ebbets Field game, "*The music rises to a mocking frenzy.*"

At the start of the restaurant scene, "*Suddenly mucous music is heard,*" which again represents the modern world and is the very opposite of the flute.

The optimistic *"gay music of the Boys is heard"* is heard again as Willy imagines himself talking with Ben about the insurance money. But as *"the car speeds off, the music crashes down in a frenzy of sound, which becomes the soft pulsation of a single cello string."* For the Requiem it morphs into *"a dead march."* As the mourners leave the graveside, *"Only the music of the flute is left on the darkening stage as over the house the hard towers of the apartment buildings rise into sharp focus, and the curtain falls."*

Minor Symbols

Willy's **sample cases** represent his role as a salesman. The audience's first sight of Willy shows him burdened by the weight of his cases and relieved to be able to set them down. The career that Willy chose as a young man has failed to fulfill the hopes he had of it. Now, he is too old and too tired to compete against rival salesmen.

The **building supplies** that Biff and Happy steal from the building site so that Willy could build a new stoop symbolize both Willy's skill in building something practical, but also his error in thinking that there are short cuts in building a future and a legacy.

Football symbolizes the promise of success and adulation in America. Willy sees it as representing the competitive world of business and assumes that, since Biff achieves outstanding success on the field, he will be able to do the same in business. When Happy wants to impress the young woman he is flirting with in the restaurant, he tells her that Biff is a quarterback with the New York giants. Ironically, this only beings home to the audience the extent to which Biff has failed to fulfill the potential that Willy saw in him.

Tennis is another symbol of success. At this time, tennis was a more upper class game that football. When Willy (and the audience) sees Bernard with a tennis racket, it represents how he has successfully raised himself socially to associate with fine people. In contrast, Biff's friends are ranch hands and Happy's friends (in so far as he can be said to have any) are the people he works with. While Biff and Happy can only look back on Biff's early success in sports and fantasize about the games The Loman Brothers will stage, Bernard actually plays sport.

The **rubber hose** is a symbol of Willy's death wish. The pipe is normally connected to the water heater, one of those modern appliances that Willy works so hard to buy and to repair when they break. Thus, like Willy's other suicide attempts, by driving off the road in the car he uses to travel to work, the hose is linked to the modern world from which Willy is increasingly alienated.

The **stockings** that Willy gives to The Woman during his affair with her symbolize Willy's betrayal of his wife and sons. When Biff discovers Willy with The Woman he tells his father accusingly, "You gave her Mama's stockings!" Thus, they become in Willy's mind a symbol of his sexual infidelity. While Linda is reduced to mending her stocking, The Woman gets new ones in return for sex. His inability to keep Linda in stockings (at that time a luxury item) is a constant reminder to Willy of his failure to provide financially for his family

The **moon**, which Willy sees at night, is a symbol of hope.

The **wire recorder** which Willy encounters in Howard's office symbolizes the advancement of technology. Willy has never seen one before, and when he accidentally turns it on, he panics because he does not know how to turn it off. Throughout the play Willy is fighting a losing battle with modern appliances that break down and cost money to get fixed; they represent a world in which he feels himself to be losing control. The business world has passed Willy by: he is more at home in a world of basic tools where he can make the things that he needs himself and make them so that they last. The recorder and the happy voices of his wife and children to which Howard insists that he listens only serve to symbolize the success that Willy has always dreamed of (both in terms of finance and family life) but has never attained.

Willy's current **car**, the Studebaker, similarly symbolizes the modern world and Willy's inability to keep the Studebaker on the road represents his wider inability to control his life. Nostalgically, he thinks back to the car he had fifteen years ago, "I coulda sworn I was driving that Chevvy" – the one where you could open the windscreen to let the air flow through. The Chevy is a symbol for the American dream at a period in Willy's life when he seemed still to be able to attain that dream. The memory of the open windshield symbolizes a time in his life when the worlds of the city and the country still seemed to be in balance. That balance has since tipped decisively in favor of the city – and against Willy.

Biff admits to having stolen three items: **a carton of basketballs, a suit and a pen**. These are all thing of material value and thus represent his desire to get ahead without actually putting in the work necessary to do so. The suit and the pen are more specifically symbols associated with success in business. Aware that he is "a dime a dozen" and will never be the success that his father predicted, Biff unconsciously steals things that symbolize that success for him (just as Happy 'steals' the women of his business superiors).

The **seeds** that Willy plants symbolize the love of nature that he inherits from his father. Ironically, he expresses his awareness that he has failed to accumulate a financial legacy to leave to his sons, in terms of nature, saying "I don't have a thing in the ground!" They also symbolize Willy's sense of his failure to nurture Biff and (to a lesser extent) Happy. The seeds represent his last, desperate attempt to leave some tangible result of a lifetime of work because Willy feels that a man should achieve something. However, as Linda gently reminds him, the surrounding buildings cut out the light so that seeds will not grow. The fact that Willy attempts to plant the seeds in the dark symbolizes his total failure to understand nature the business world in which he is living.

Diamonds represent to Willy tangible wealth; they are a form of wealth that a man can literally hold in his hand. In so far as his brother Ben attained this form of wealth, while Willy conspicuously does not, they symbolize Willy's failure as a salesman and the failure of the American Dream to deliver on its promise of financial security. Willy firmly believes that "a man has got to add up to something." Finally, Willy deludes himself that by suicide he will get the diamonds that his brother got in the form of the insurance money and so make his life meaningful. He imagines Ben telling him that "the jungle is dark but full of diamonds." In deciding to commit suicide, Willy perceives himself as emulating Ben by going into the jungle to get a legacy for Biff.

Literary Terms

NOTE: Not every one of these terms will be equally relevant to this particular study guide

Ambiguous, ambiguity: when a statement is unclear in meaning – ambiguity may be deliberate or accidental.

Analogy: a comparison which treats two things as identical in one or more specified ways.

Antagonist: a character or force opposing the protagonist.

Antithesis: the complete opposite of something.

Climax: the conflict to which the action has been building since the start of the play or story.

Colloquialism: the casual, informal mainly spoken language of ordinary people – often called "slang."

Connotation: the ideas, feelings and associations generated by a word or phrase.

Dark comedy: comedy which has a serious implication – comedy that deals with subjects not usually treated humorously (e.g., death).

Dialogue: a conversation between two or more people in direct speech.

Diction: the writer's choice of words in order to create a particular effect.

Equivocation: saying something which is capable of two interpretations with the intention of misrepresenting the truth.

Euphemism: a polite word for an ugly truth – for example, a person is said to be sleeping when they are actually dead.

Fallacy: a misconception resulting from incorrect reasoning.

Foreshadowing: a statement or action which gives the reader a hint of what is likely to happen later in the narrative.

Genre: the type of literature into which a particular text falls (e.g. drama, poetry, novel).

Image, imagery: figurative language such as simile, metaphor, personification etc., or a description which conjures up a particularly vivid picture.

Imply, implication: when the text suggests to the reader a meaning which it does not actually state.

Infer, inference: the reader's act of going beyond what is stated in the text to draw conclusions.

Irony, ironic: a form of humor which undercuts the apparent meaning of a statement:

Conscious irony: irony used deliberately by a writer or character;
Unconscious irony: a statement or action which has significance for the reader of which the character is unaware;
Dramatic irony: when an action has an important significance that is obvious to the reader but not to one or more of the characters;
Tragic irony: when a character says (or does) something which will have a serious, even fatal, consequence for him/ her. The audience is aware of the error, but the character is not;
Verbal irony: the conscious use of particular words which are appropriate to what is being said.
Juxtaposition: literally putting two things side by side for purposes of comparison and/ or contrast.
Literal: the surface level of meaning that a statement has.
Melodramatic: action and/or dialogue that is inflated or extravagant – frequently used for comic effect.
Metaphor, metaphorical: the description of one thing by direct comparison with another (e.g. the coal-black night). Extended metaphor: a comparison which is developed at length.
Mood: the feelings and emotions contained in and/ or produced by a work of art (text, painting, music, etc.).
Motif: a frequently repeated idea, image or situation in a text.
Motivation: why a character acts as he/she does – in modern literature motivation is seen as psychological.
Oxymoron: the juxtaposition of two terms normally thought of as opposite (e.g. the silent scream).
Paradox, paradoxical: a statement or situation which appears self-contradictory and therefore absurd.
Pathos: is pity, or rather the ability of a text to make the audience or reader feel pity.
Perspective: point of view from which a story, or an incident within a story, is told.
Personified, personification: a simile or metaphor in which an inanimate object or abstract idea is described by comparison with a human.
Plot: a chain of events linked by cause and effect.
Protagonist: the character who initiates the action and is most likely to have the sympathy of the audience.
Realism: a text that describes the action in a way that appears to reflect life.

Rhetoric: any use of language designed to make the expression of ideas more effective (e.g. repetition, imagery, alliteration, etc.).

Sarcasm: stronger than irony – it involves a deliberate attack on a person or idea with the intention of mocking.

Setting: the environment in which the narrative (or part of the narrative) takes place.

Simile: a description of one thing by explicit comparison with another (e.g. my love is like a red, red rose). Extended simile: a comparison which is developed at length.

Style: the way in which a writer chooses to express him/ herself. Style is a vital aspect of meaning since how something is expressed can crucially affect what is being written or spoken.

Suspense: the building of tension in the reader.

Symbol, symbolic, symbolism, symbolize: a physical object which comes to represent an abstract idea (e.g. the sun may symbolize life).

Themes: important concepts, beliefs and ideas explored and presented in a text.

Third person: third person singular is "he/ she/ it" and plural is "they" – authors often write novels in the third person.

Tone: literally the sound of a text – How words sound (either in the mouth of an actor or the head of a reader) can crucially affect meaning.

Tragic: King Richard III and Macbeth are both murderous tyrants, yet only Macbeth is a tragic figure. Why? Because Macbeth has the potential to be great, recognizes the error he has made and all that he has lost in making it, and dies bravely in a way that seems to accept the justice of the punishment.

Literary Terms Activity

As you use each term in the study guide, fill in the definition of the term and include an example from the text to show how it is used. The first definition is supplied. Find an example in the text to complete it.

Term	Definition
	Example
Ambiguous, ambiguity	*when a statement is unclear in meaning- ambiguity may be deliberate or accidental*
Foreshadowing	
Image/imagery	
Dramatic irony	
Metaphor/ metaphorical	
Symbolism	

Term	Definition
	Example

Graphic Organizers

Plot

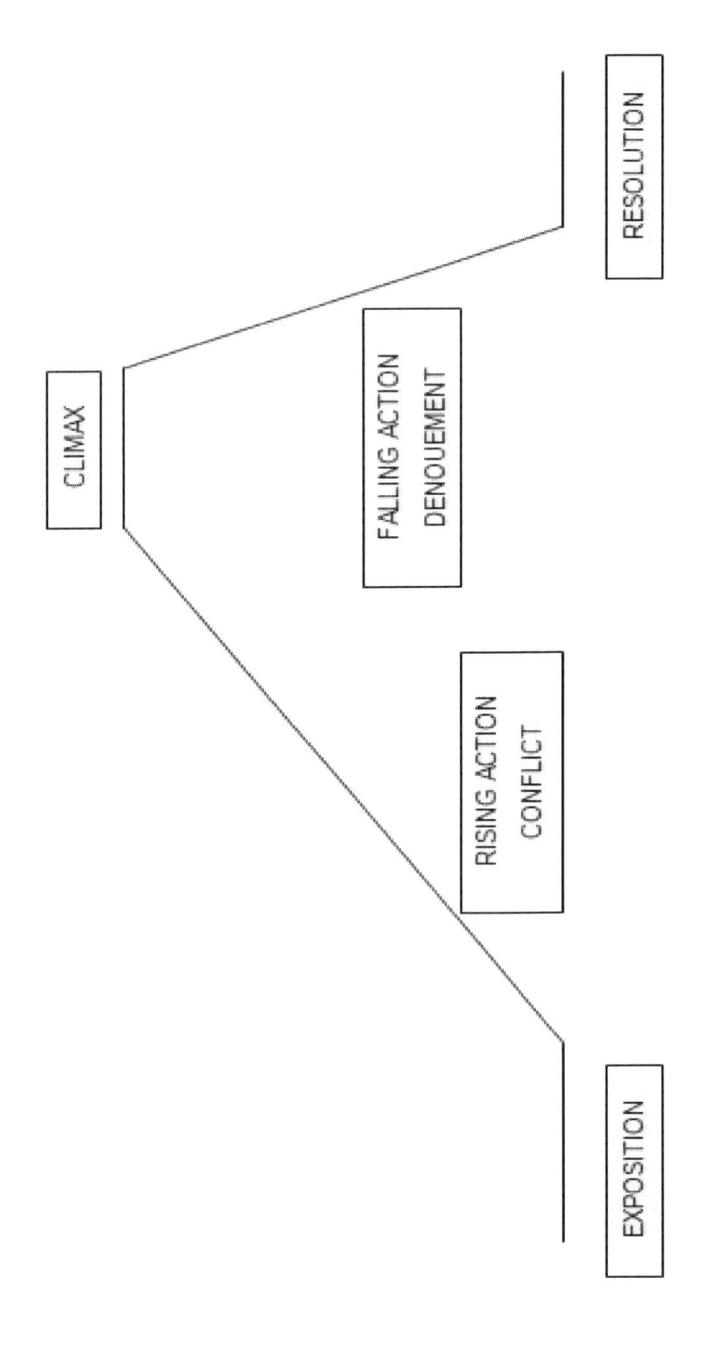

```
                                                    RESOLUTION
            CLIMAX
                    FALLING ACTION
                    DENOUEMENT

                RISING ACTION
                CONFLICT

                                    EXPOSITION
```

Different perspectives

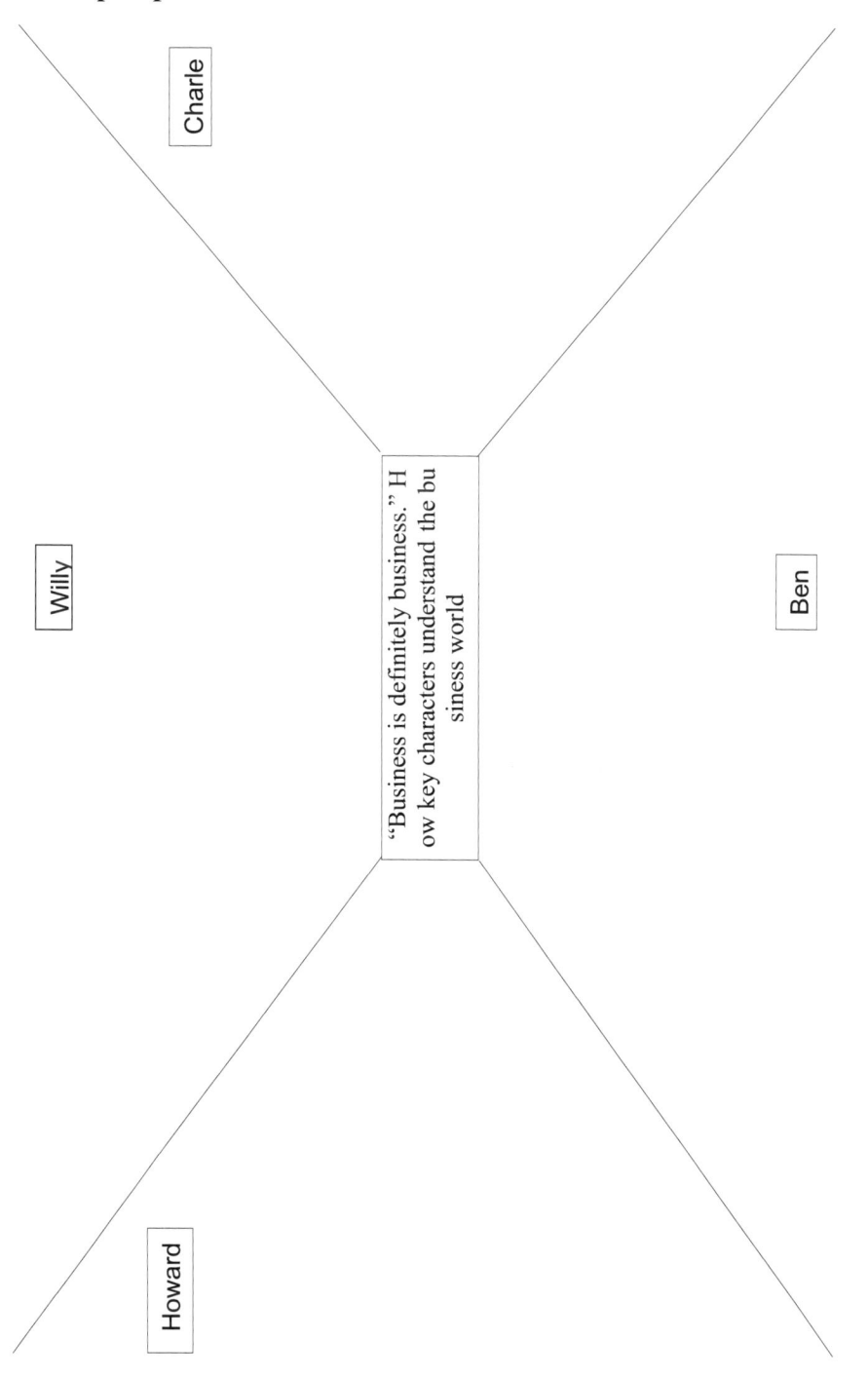

Charley

Willy

Ben

"Business is definitely business." How key characters understand the business world

Howard

Reading Group Use of the Study Guide Questions

Although there are both closed and open questions in the Study Guide, very few of them have simple, right or wrong answers. They are designed to encourage in-depth discussion, disagreement, and (eventually) consensus. Above all, they aim to encourage readers to go to the text to support their conclusions and interpretations.

I am not so arrogant as to presume to tell readers how they should use this resource. I used it in the following ways, each of which ensured that group members were well prepared for group discussion and presentations.

1. Set a reading assignment for the group and tell everyone to be aware that the questions will be the focus of whole group discussion at the next meeting.

2. Set a reading assignment for the group and allocate particular questions to sections of the group (e.g. if there are four questions, divide the group into four sections, etc.).

In the meeting, form discussion groups containing one person who has prepared each question and allow time for feedback within the groups.

Have feedback to the whole the on each question by picking a group at random to present their answers and to follow up with a group discussion.

3. Set a reading assignment for the group, but do not allocate questions.

In the meeting, divide readers into groups and allocate to each group one of the questions related to the reading assignment, the answer to which they will have to present formally to the meeting.

Allow time for discussion and preparation.

4. Set a reading assignment for the group, but do not allocate questions.

In the meeting, divide readers into groups and allocate to each group one of the questions related to the reading assignment.

Allow time for discussion and preparation.

Now reconfigure the groups so that each group contains at least one person who has prepared each question and allow time for feedback within the groups.

5. Before starting to read the text, allocate specific questions to individuals or pairs. (It is best not to allocate all questions to allow for other approaches and variety. One in three questions or one in four seems about right.) Tell readers that they will be leading the group discussion on their question. They will need to start with a brief presentation of the issues and then conduct a question and answer session. After this, they will be expected to present a brief review of the discussion.

6. Having finished the text, arrange the meeting into groups of 3, 4 or 5. Tell each group to select as many questions from the Study Guide as there are members of the group.

Each individual is responsible for drafting out an answer to one question, and each answer should be substantial.

Each group as a whole is then responsible for discussing, editing and suggesting improvements to each answer.

Bibliography

The Miller literature is vast and I make no claim to have done more than scratch the surface. These are my main sources.

The Play

Miller, Arthur. *The Viking Critical Library: "Death of a Salesman": Text and Criticism*. Gerald Weales, ed. London: Penguin Books, 1977. Print.

Criticism

Bigsby, Christopher, ed. *The Cambridge Companion to Arthur Miller*. Second edition. Cambridge: Cambridge UP, 2010. Print.

Bloom, Harold. ed. *Bloom's Guides: Arthur Miller's 'Death of a Salesman'*. New York: Chelsea House, 2004. Print.

---. *Major Literary Characters: Willy Loman*. New York: Chelsea House, 1991. Print.

---. *Modern Critical Interpretations: Arthur Miller's 'Death of a Salesman'*. New York: Chelsea House, 1988. Print.

Griffin, Alice. Understanding Arthur Miller. Columbia, University of South Carolina, 1996. Print.

Lerner, Alicia, and Adrienne Lerner, ed. *Social Issues in Literature: Suicide in Arthur Miller's 'Death of a Salesman'*. Detroit: Greenhaven Press, 2008. Print

Moss, Leonard. *Arthur Miller*. Boston: Twayne Publishers, 1980. Print.

Scheidt, Jennifer L. *CliffsNotes on 'Death of a Salesman'*. Web. 05 Jul 2018.

Siebold, Thomas, ed. *Readings on Arthur Miller*. San Diego: Greenhaven Press, 1997. Print.

---, *Readings on 'Death of a Salesman'*. San Diego: Greenhaven Press, 1999. Print.

SparkNotes Editors. "SparkNote on *Death of a Salesman*." SparkNotes.com. SparkNotes LLC. 2002. Web. 20 Sept. 2018.

To the Reader

Ray Moore was born in Nottingham, England. He obtained his Master's Degree in Literature from Lancaster University and taught in secondary education for twenty-eight years before relocating to Florida with his wife. There he taught English and Information Technology in the International Baccalaureate Program at a Florida High School. He is now a full-time writer and fitness fanatic.

Website: http://www.raymooreauthor.com

Ray strives to make his texts the best that they can be. If you have any comments or question about this book please contact the author through his email: villageswriter@gmail.com

Also by Ray Moore:

All books are available from amazon.com and from barnesandnoble.com as paperbacks and at most online eBook retailers.

Fiction:

The Lyle Thorne Mysteries: each book features five tales from the Golden Age of Detection:

   Investigations of The Reverend Lyle Thorne
   Further Investigations of The Reverend Lyle Thorne
   Early Investigations of Lyle Thorne
   Sanditon Investigations of The Reverend Lyle Thorne
   Final Investigations of The Reverend Lyle Thorne
   Lost Investigations of The Reverend Lyle Thorne
   Official Investigations of Lyle Thorne

Non-fiction:

The Critical Introduction series is written for high school teachers and students and for college undergraduates. Each volume gives an in-depth analysis of a key text:

   "The General Prologue" by Geoffrey Chaucer: A Critical Introduction
   "The Great Gatsby" by F. Scott Fitzgerald: A Critical Introduction
   "Pride and Prejudice" by Jane Austen: A Critical Introduction
   "The Stranger" by Albert Camus: A Critical Introduction (Revised Second Edition)

The Text and Critical Introduction series differs from the Critical introduction series as these books contain the original text and in the case of the medieval texts an interlinear translation to aid the understanding of the text. The commentary allows the reader to develop a deeper understanding of the text and themes within the text.

"Sir Gawain and the Green Knight": Text and Critical Introduction
"The General Prologue" by Geoffrey Chaucer: Text and Critical Introduction
"Heart of Darkness" by Joseph Conrad: Text and Critical Introduction
"Henry V" by William Shakespeare: Text and Critical Introduction
"Oedipus Rex" by Sophocles: Text and Critical Introduction
"A Room with a View" By E.M. Forster: Text and Critical Introduction
"The Sign of Four" by Sir Arthur Conan Doyle Text and Critical Introduction
"The Wife of Bath's Prologue and Tale" by Geoffrey Chaucer: Text and Critical Introduction

Study guides available in print - listed alphabetically by author

* denotes also available as an eBook

"ME and EARL and the Dying GIRL" by Jesse Andrews: A Study Guide
Study Guide to "Alias Grace" by Margaret Atwood
Study Guide to "The Handmaid's Tale" by Margaret Atwood*
"Pride and Prejudice" by Jane Austen: A Study Guide
"Moloka'i" by Alan Brennert: A Study Guide
"Wuthering Heights" by Emily Brontë: A Study Guide *
"Jane Eyre" by Charlotte Brontë: A Study Guide *
"The Stranger" by Albert Camus: A Study Guide
"The Myth of Sisyphus" by Albert Camus: A Study Guide
"The Myth of Sisyphus" and "The Stranger" by Albert Camus: Two Study Guides *
Study Guide to "Death Comes to the Archbishop" by Willa Cather
"The Awakening" by Kate Chopin: A Study Guide
Study Guide to "Seven Short Stories" by Kate Chopin
Study Guide to "Ready Player One" by Ernest Cline
Study Guide to "Disgrace" by J. M. Coetzee
"The Meursault Investigation" by Kamel Daoud: A Study Guide
Study Guide on "Great Expectations" by Charles Dickens*
"The Sign of Four" by Sir Arthur Conan Doyle: A Study Guide *
"The Wasteland, Prufrock and Poems" by T.S. Eliot: A Study Guide
Study Guide to "Manhattan Beach" by Jennifer Egan
Study Guide to "Birdsong" by Sebastian Faulks*
"The Great Gatsby" by F. Scott Fitzgerald: A Study Guide

"A Room with a View" by E. M. Forster: A Study Guide
"Looking for Alaska" by John Green: A Study Guide
"Paper Towns" by John Green: A Study Guide
Study Guide to "Turtles All The Way Down" by John Green
"Catch-22" by Joseph Heller: A Study Guide *
"Unbroken" by Laura Hillenbrand: A Study Guide
"The Kite Runner" by Khaled Hosseini: A Study Guide
"A Thousand Splendid Suns" by Khaled Hosseini: A Study Guide
"The Secret Life of Bees" by Sue Monk Kidd: A Study Guide
Study Guide on "The Invention of Wings" by Sue Monk Kidd
"Go Set a Watchman" by Harper Lee: A Study Guide
"On the Road" by Jack Keruoac: A Study Guide
Study Guide to "Fear and Trembling" by Soren Kierkegaard
Study Guide to "Pachinko" by Min Jin Lee
"Life of Pi" by Yann Martel: A Study Guide *
Study Guide to "The Bluest Eye" by Toni Morrison
Study Guide to "Reading Lolita in Tehran" by Azar Nafisi
"Animal Farm" by George Orwell: A Study Guide
Study Guide on "Nineteen Eighty-Four" by George Orwell
Study Guide to "Selected Poems" and Additional Poems by Sylvia Plath*
"An Inspector Calls" by J.B. Priestley: A Study Guide
Study Guide to "Cross Creek" by Marjorie Kinnan Rawlings
"Esperanza Rising" by Pam Munoz Ryan: A Study Guide
"The Catcher in the Rye" by J.D. Salinger: A Study Guide
"Where'd You Go, Bernadette" by Maria Semple: A Study Guide
"Henry V" by William Shakespeare: A Study Guide
Study Guide on "Macbeth" by William Shakespeare *
"Othello" by William Shakespeare: A Study Guide *
"Antigone" by Sophocles: A Study Guide*
"Oedipus Rex" by Sophocles: A Study Guide
"Cannery Row" by John Steinbeck: A Study Guide
"East of Eden" by John Steinbeck: A Study Guide
"The Grapes of Wrath" by John Steinbeck: A Study Guide
"Of Mice and Men" by John Steinbeck: A Study Guide*
"The Goldfinch" by Donna Tartt: A Study Guide
"Walden; or, Life in the Woods" by Henry David Thoreau: A Study Guide
Study Guide to "Cat's Cradle" by Kurt Vonnegut

"The Bridge of San Luis Rey" by Thornton Wilder: A Study Guide *
Study Guide on "The Book Thief" by Markus Zusak

Study Guides available as e-books:
Study Guide on "Heart of Darkness" by Joseph Conrad
Study Guide on "The Mill on the Floss" by George Eliot
Study Guide on "Lord of the Flies" by William Golding
Study Guide on "Nineteen Eighty-Four" by George Orwell
Study Guide on "Henry IV Part 2" by William Shakespeare
Study Guide on "Julius Caesar" by William Shakespeare
Study Guide on "The Pearl" by John Steinbeck
Study Guide on "Slaughterhouse-Five" by Kurt Vonnegut

New titles are added regularly.

Teacher resources:

Ray also publishes many more study guides and other resources for classroom use on the 'Teachers Pay Teachers' website:
http://www.teacherspayteachers.com/Store/Raymond-Moore

Printed in Great Britain
by Amazon